Writing Tasks

An authentic-task approach
to individual writing needs

Teacher's Book

David Jolly

CAMBRIDGE
UNIVERSITY PRESS

Published by the Press Syndicate of the University of Cambridge
The Pitt Building, Trumpington Street, Cambridge CB2 1RP
40 West 20th Street, New York, NY 10011-4211, USA
10 Stamford Road, Oakleigh, Victoria 3166, Australia

© Cambridge University Press 1984

First published 1984
Sixth printing 1992

Printed in Great Britain
at The Bath Press, Avon

ISBN 0 521 28972 6 Teacher's Book
ISBN 0 521 22924 3 Student's Book

Copyright

BS

Contents

Contents

Acknowledgements

I would like to take this opportunity to thank Adrian at Cambridge University Press for encouraging the book in the first place, and my editors Christine, Kay, Geraldine and Alison, who have all been exceptionally kind and patient with me. I would also like to thank past and present colleagues and students at South Devon Technical College and Exeter College for use of and comment on the materials contained in this book. Finally, a word of quiet appreciation for all the many people I live with for tolerating a great deal of noise from a very old typewriter.

The author and publishers are grateful to the authors, publishers and others who have given permission for the use of copyright material identified in the text. It has not been possible to identify the sources of all the material used and in such cases the publishers would welcome information from copyright owners.
Unicliffe and Sharps Advertising Ltd for the illustrations on pp. 66, 67 and 68; Wiggins Teape Carbonless Paper for the form on p. 103; Selective Marketplace for the form on p. 104; Bwrdd Croeso Cymru Wales Tourist Board for the form on p. 105; Barclays Bank PLC for the cheque on p. 106; Irwin Lowen, Senior Vice President, SAI Group for the form on p. 107; Time Assurance Society and Ansvar Insurance Co Ltd for the forms on p. 108; Sun Alliance Insurance Group for the form on p. 109; Rediffusion Music for the advertisement on p. 114; RMC Homecare Ltd for the advertisement on p. 115; Ministry of Defence for the article on p. 144; Geraldine Stoneham for the short story on p. 163.

Illustrations by Chris Evans, Annie McManus and Trevor Ridley; artwork by Amandrew Studios
Book design by Peter Ducker MSTD

To the teacher

The Teacher's Book for *Writing Tasks* has two functions. It supplies explanatory notes for the writing materials as a whole, and also for the constituent parts; it supplies reproducible ancillary materials in the form of exercises and further task practices, and also tests. A key to the exercises appears at the end of the book.

The general introduction offers a teaching rationale for the contents and their use, explains ways in which students and teachers may use the materials, and shows teachers how *Writing Tasks* may be adapted for use in their own classroom.

After the introduction, each of the seven writing sections is dealt with in turn. An introduction to each kind of writing explains the functional uses of each writing type; there is also a brief description of the rhetorical conventions governing such writing and, where possible or relevant, a short description of some of the linguistic features involved. These notes should be read in conjunction with the introductions for each unit in the Student's Book. Each section then deals with the units in that section one by one. There is a brief unit introduction, exercises, further practice items and tests – although not all units follow the same pattern. The unit material should be looked at in conjunction with the material for each unit in the Student's Book. At the end of the Teacher's Book there is a key to the language exercises and also model answers for Unit 7.3.

As a teacher, you have our permission to reproduce the exercise, practice and test materials contained in this book for use within your school or college.

To the student who uses this book

If you do not attend an English language class and do not have a regular English teacher, you will need to use this book to gain access to the exercises, extra practices and key. You will, however, still need a teacher, or competent English-speaking person to mark your work.

N.B.   To avoid having to repeat 'he or she' each time the question of the sex of the teacher or student arises, I have chosen to use the general form 'he'. This is not to suggest that all students and teachers are male, but is used only for the sake of convenience.

Introduction

A rationale for *Writing Tasks*

The decision that an individual makes to write something, whether the 'something' is a note to the milkman or an anecdotal letter to a friend, is made as the result of social pressures, impulses or circumstances. Furthermore, the reason for writing directs what is written, and the manner in which it is written.

For this reason, the seven sections of this book and the forty units that are contained within them have been arranged with reference to the social uses of writing (for example, giving information to people you don't have the time or opportunity to see personally; buying things by filling in forms; reporting experience to acquaintances) rather than with reference to the meanings that can be expressed in written English, or the grammatical forms needed to express such meanings.

In a book dealing with writing, clear suggestions can be made about textual form, style and functional language. Much vaguer help can be offered at the content level since content language arises out of particular contexts. Thus, in one particular instance, the predictable social skill of being able to write a personal letter is dependent upon the unpredictable language skills of being able to express accurate time relations, the concept of lateness and so on. In another instance, however, the necessary language skills may be entirely different. A book that attempted to deal comprehensively with the written expression of all notions available in English would be impossibly large.

Therefore, while the acquisition of structural and notional skills is extremely important to successful writing, the practice of writing as a social skill that *Writing Tasks* provides at a whole-text level, is equally vital to writing good English texts. Thus the purpose of this book is to develop students' ability to write whole texts using the appropriate form, style and language, by offering authentic models and functional practice at text-type level.

In doing this, then, there are two major functions that *Writing Tasks* fulfils. First, to quote Widdowson and Davies, 'it would seem that the real difficulty associated with writing is to be traced to the communication stage ... writing is a social activity of a rather specialist and restricted kind, and to learn to write is to learn a kind of social behaviour.'[1] The second is supported by Chris Brumfit's delineation of the alternative view of the teaching–learning cycle.[2] In this view, practice of the language (at the language skills level) arises out of student and teacher observation of performance by the student in a communicative task. Therefore the 'open plan' structure of the *Writing Tasks* course contributes to this practice. An adaptation of the Brumfit model would appear as follows:

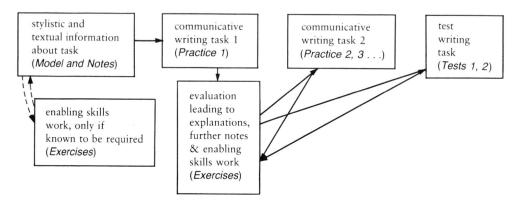

The stages contained in the diagram (Model, Practice, Exercises) relate to stages in each section in this material. The role of the teacher in this model of language learning will be commented on at greater length on page 9 of this introduction, particularly the importance of the teacher as an evaluator.

What the books contain

The Student's Book is divided into seven functional areas. The first three (1: Writing notes and memos, 2: Writing personal letters, and 3: Writing telegrams etc.) and the last two (6: Writing to companies and officials, and 7: Presenting facts, ideas and opinions) are whole text-types in themselves; Sections 4 (Writing descriptions) and 5 (Reporting experiences) may be included as parts of other texts. For example, a description could stand by itself or be incorporated in a letter.

Each section has an introduction. The sections are further subdivided into a number of single units according to the function of the writing.

1 Widdowson, H. and Davies, N. F., 'Reading and writing', *Techniques in Applied Linguistics*, The Edinburgh Course in Applied Linguistics, Vol. 3 ed. J. B. P. Allen and S. Pit Corder, 1976.
2 Brumfit, C. 'Accuracy and fluency as polarities in foreign language materials and methodology' 1979 Bulletin CILA number 29, pp. 89–99.

The composition of the units varies but the underlying pattern of the materials is as follows:
– there are *models* of the kind of text that students may wish to write.
– accompanying the models are explanatory *notes* on textual use, style and writing conventions.
– in most units there are *language notes* containing guidance to the sort of language used.
– a set of instructions called *What to do* tells the student how to proceed through the unit.
– following this there are a number of practices based on real-life situations.

The Teacher's Book contains:
– a sample checklist.
– exercise materials available for some units.
– further practice materials available for most units.
– two tests for each unit (with a couple of exceptions).
There is also an introduction to each section and an introductory note to each unit. At the end of the book there is a key to the exercises.

Using the book

The materials and methodology of *Writing Tasks* have been developed with the upper-intermediate and more advanced student in mind. They can be used below that level if great care is taken in restricting access to certain units; naturally there is no upper limit to the competence of the user since the materials require students to complete real-life tasks.

The materials can be used for short intensive courses or long non-intensive courses but teachers should read the notes under the heading 'Writing Tasks and classroom work' below, for guidance.

A personal syllabus for students

On page 1 of the Student's Book, some suggestions have been made to students about drawing up their own personal writing scheme: why they should do it and how they can go about it. You should read this section in conjunction with the notes in the Student's Book.

WHY?

A number of recent approaches to the teaching of English as a foreign language have placed the learner at the centre of learning (rather than focusing on the teacher or upon systems). Some of these approaches

have placed strong emphasis upon self-expression *per se*, particularly
in the approach to speaking and listening skills. When it comes to
writing in a foreign language, however, my own experience leads me
to believe that most foreign-language learners do not have very much
inclination to write for self-expression in the languages they are
learning; in fact, I would go further and suggest that a lot of learners
would happily dispense with writing entirely. Widdowson and Davies,
in writing on this subject had this to say of the native speaker: 'What
kind of social activity is writing? Perhaps the first thing to note is that
it is a reasonably rare one. Most people do little or no writing . . .
Writing is a normal social activity for the professional minority, who
produce institutional writing, and for a small number of people who
produce the occasional personal writing.'[1] If this view, that the
majority of native language users do not write (or apparently do not
need to) in their own language, is valid, the foreign-language teacher
needs to be careful about the demands he makes on his students.

The origins of the present book, and its content and style, reflect
this view. Most students of English are able to recognise quite clear
and specific learning needs when it comes to writing; or, if not specific
needs, at least an awareness of what may or may not be useful either
at the time of learning or in the future. Some students, a small
minority, have a desire to write for pleasure or simple self-expression
in a foreign language.

Given the disparities in learning objectives that reveal themselves
in a single group of students, it seems clear that a set of materials
organised on a self-access basis is more valuable than the traditional
whole class approach where everyone works on the same thing at the
same time.

HOW?

The idea of a student creating his own scheme of work, independent
of you, his teacher, may seem disturbingly novel. It may also be very
difficult for the student to do this at first: students are so used to
having no influence at all on what is studied, or how, or when, or
where, that the proffered freedom may paralyse. In John Holt's
pungent image, the lion cannot jump when the hoop is taken away.
Students faced with this freedom will need a lot of encouragement,
both in deciding initially what needs and wants they may have, and
then in relating these to a coherent and continuing writing
programme for themselves.

Writing tasks and classroom work

However, despite what has been said above about students developing

1 *ibid.*

their own programmes of work, it may be necessary for some students and some classes to receive guidance from their class teacher, either because students find it initially difficult to take control of their own learning, or, more practically, because there are clear pedagogical grounds for doing so. Of the latter we may distinguish two sorts:

i) you may know for certain that your students do not have the language skills to tackle certain units (e.g. 7.3 Summary report writing demands quite sophisticated abilities),

ii) you may wish to delay access to certain units until you have done some related oral work in class. It should be understood here that this is not to suggest that there are any *a priori* reasons why writing should follow oral work or vice versa; but it is clear that for some sections (notably Section 4: Writing descriptions, and Section 5: Reporting experiences) this approach could yield notable benefits for writing. In contrast, other sections (e.g. Section 3) reveal no very meaningful relationship between speech and writing.

It may be useful at this point to offer a few examples of restricted-access syllabuses for particular groups of students to illustrate what is meant.

1 The teacher who has a general upper-intermediate group of students on an intensive course may decide to restrict access to the writing materials to the following:
Section 1 (all) Section 2 (all) Section 3 (3.1 and 3.2) Section 4 (not 4.5) Section 5 (5.1 and 5.2) Section 6 (6.1 and 6.2) Section 7 (7.1)

2 The teacher who has a non-intensive class over a period of one or two years, may decide that he wants to offer all the material to his students, but that he wants to link some of the units to later oral work, and hold back other units because he feels that they will be coped with best near the end of the course. A syllabus might then be broken down into four sections: A (first 6 months), A and B (second 6 months), A, B and C (third 6 months), and A, B, C and D (the last 6 months).

A: Section 1 (all)
   Section 2 (2.1/2.2/2.3/2.7)
   Section 6 (6.1/6.2)

C: Section 2 (2.8)
   Section 4 (4.1/4.3/4.4/4.6/4.7)
   Section 6 (6.3/6.4)
   Section 7 (7.1/7.4)

B: Section 2 (2.4/2.5/2.6)
   Section 3 (all)
   Section 4 (4.2/4.5)
   Section 5 (5.1/5.2/5.4)
   Section 6 (6.5/6.6/6.7)
D: Section 2 (2.9)
   Section 5 (5.3)
   Section 7 (7.2/7.3/7.5)

3 The third example is of the teacher who is taking an examination class and who may decide to restrict his students' syllabus to those

types of writing that are asked for in the examination; in this case, old exam questions become extra practice items for the students.

More will be said on the relation between these materials and classroom work in the section on *Exercises* below.

How to use a unit: Student's Book

INTRODUCTIONS TO SECTIONS

These introductions in the Student's Book contain information about the text-types in each section, and include notes on style, use, and language. Students are asked to read these for themselves, but it may be valuable to go through these introductions with groups of students who are going to be involved in using the same sections. The introductions also offer more explicit information to the student about the nature of the different units in any one section than is available from the writing checklist. This is very important since in any self-access system the problems of metalanguage (i.e. language which describes language!) can be a barrier to effective student choice and decision-making.

For each unit, the student will find models and practices.

MODELS

The approach used in *Writing Tasks* is one that has become more familiar in textbooks for writing recently; the writing of whole texts is based on the reading of whole texts, usually authentic texts. These have replaced specially-written examples which were designed to show off language items. It is never actually possible to provide the foreign language learner with sufficient model texts to allow him to assimilate the necessary facts of language, style and appropriacy that make the path to good writing an easier one for the native user of the language. The foreign learner must rely upon one or two aptly-chosen models, summarising notes, and then, correction from teachers. It is as well then to encourage students not to regard the models offered with each unit as sacrosanct or infinitely reproducible. The models offer some indications of the bounds of a certain text-type, not definitive and comprehensive versions, and they should not be slavishly imitated when students come to write their own texts.

The models in *Writing Tasks* contain language notes. In some units, the level of linguistic prediction can be quite high; for example, in writing letters of request to companies or officials (6.2) one can be fairly confident of setting down most of the request forms and their variations. However, in the majority of cases the language notes are just that: notes, not teaching presentations or exercises. This is not to say that no help at these levels has been given; where appropriate and possible, the notes appended to the models are amplified in the Teacher's Book, and in certain units, exercises to be used by the teacher, or given to the students are included in the Teacher's Book.

It is important that the teacher using these materials has a clear idea about the kind of language appropriate to each unit text-type and has the resources to deal with language problems as they arise (resources actually in the Teacher's Book, as well as resources from other textbooks or personal materials).

At the end of each model section there is a paragraph of outline instructions entitled *What to do*. The instructions will guide the student through each unit as he tackles it, and also include references to materials in the Teacher's Book.

PRACTICES

Every effort has been made to create authentic contexts as incentives to the writing of texts. The practices do not, therefore, require the students to write commercial advertisements, pop-songs or school reports. They attempt to anticipate the kinds of social situations that foreign students might find themselves faced with, and in which there is a pressure (desire or need) to write. This is less easy in Sections 4 and 5 where the kinds of writing practised do not so readily relate to particular text-types or writing situations. For example, authentic contexts for describing things (4.3) may be found in reports, small ads, personal letters, and so on.

Teacher's Book

EXERCISES

The exercises associated with particular units have been placed in the Teacher's Book for two reasons:
i)   they may not be necessary for every student to do,
ii) the teacher who uses these materials may have better or more suitable materials, or may wish to combine these exercises with his own.

Quite a number of the units are concerned with a student's ability to express content which cannot possibly be predicted with any certainty by a third party. Units involving reporting and describing can only suggest general semantic areas that students might find useful in writing texts. Therefore, only the most obvious practice of language items in relation to specific units has been included. This approach differs from other writing textbooks which adopt the view that semantic and grammatical exercise work can be interwoven in an arbitrary way with functional and text-type units.

As teachers mark their students' work they will obviously come across a very broad cross-section of error, both inaccuracies and inappropriacies, that could not have been anticipated in this book. Thus, such exercises as do appear in the Teacher's Book can only be seen as part of the repertoire of language skills practice that teachers might be expected to have at their disposal.

The decision whether to tackle the exercise material or not is best taken jointly by student and teacher. On the other hand, the teacher using this book may decide to use these exercises at class level, before students get round to handling relevant writing tasks in the Student's Book.

FURTHER PRACTICES

Not all units have further practices in the Teacher's Book. Further practice items have been placed in the Teacher's Book where experience has shown that some students require a lot of practice to achieve an accurate and acceptable level of writing performance (as in Unit 1.5   Apologies and explanations).

TESTS

It has been suggested on page 5 of the Student's Book that students should ask to take tests when they feel ready to do so. This depends on whether the student, in consultation with his teacher, feels that he is capable of writing good texts alone in a particular unit. The reasons for taking tests then are quite straightforward: (i) for the student to find out whether in fact he can write certain kinds of text unaided (ii) for the teacher to find out whether students can write texts unaided.

However, in keeping with the demand for authenticity that this book makes, *tests* should be seen in their relation to real-life performance rather than classroom versions of public examinations.

For this reason, it is important that students have access to everything they would use if writing a real-life text, i.e. textbooks, reference books, dictionaries, and their own marked work. It also means that there should be no time limit for completion of the test. The difference between practices and tests, therefore, would only be that the student loses the collaborative help of his fellow students and teacher.

Of course, teachers or students may wish to use the tests as examination practice and in this case the usual examination constraints should apply; aids should be dispensed with and tests done in the dark!

KEY

At the back of the Teacher's Book there is a key to all the exercises, and also model summaries for the practices in Unit 7.3.

The teacher's role

EXPLAINING AND ADVISING

Using *Writing Tasks* as self-access materials will mean that you lose your controlling function for the writing class. But the task of persuading your students to take over this function may be very difficult, particularly in the school environment. Students will need help in deciding on writing priorities as related to their interests and needs; and will then need help in carrying through a clear writing programme. Each student in a class will require advice for his own writing problems.

KEEPING RECORDS

On page 2 of the Student's Book, suggestions have been made on how students can keep a check on their own work, using either the writing checklist on page 6 of the Student's Book, or using a checklist that you, the teacher, have devised, if you have decided to draw up a different scheme of work for your students.

It is important that you also keep a check on your students' work, perhaps using a similar sort of notation as that suggested in the Student's Book, page 3. Unlike a class situation, where the teacher controls everything that goes on in the classroom, an open-access system to materials will mean that students in any one group will be doing very different things at the same time, and will be working at very different speeds. Some students may well be working simultaneously on two or three units. Therefore, a meticulous record of what each student has done, and what needs to be redone, is essential for an effective use of *Writing Tasks*.

Students aren't always the best record-keepers of their work so your own student records may have to serve a double function from time to time, keeping both you and individual students in the picture about where they are in their writing programmes.

MARKING

This always brings out the beast in the language teacher. A well-intentioned teacher may have decided to work with a text-type and functional/notional syllabus – authentic settings, texts, and tasks, and clear goal of teaching for communicative competence. This same teacher, faced with an uncertain student text, hovers ravenously over it with the poised red pencil before descending to abolish every error in sight regardless of source of error or whether or not the errors obscure communicative effectiveness.

The Royal Society of Arts have recognised this problem in their communicative examinations by stating that only one of the criteria by which their candidates are judged is that of *accuracy*, and this criterion is modified by these explanations: (at the Basic level) 'Grammar may be shaky but what the candidate writes is intelligible and unambiguous' and (at the Intermediate level) 'Grammatical, lexical and orthographical accuracy is generally high, though some errors which do not destroy communication are acceptable . . . ' Both statements reveal a commitment to the primacy of communicative effectiveness in writing, although not at the expense of formal accuracy.

In marking students' written texts then, teachers need to be able to make useful distinctions; the table below may help:

criteria for error	*source of error*
acceptability	syntax/morphology (grammar)
	semantics (logical relations)
	reference (semantic structure reference relations)
appropriacy	textual (text-type and function)
	stylistic (social status)

A second way of looking at distinguishing errors in relation to using *Writing Tasks* may be by seeing that there is a difference between an ability to handle text-types successfully and the functions attached to them, on the one hand; and the ability to use propositional language to report, describe, and present ideas and facts about the world on the other. The latter is not necessarily related to or excluded from the writing of any particular text-type, though there may be stronger links with some text-types than with others.

You may like to study these two examples of student writing below and the accompanying marking notes to see how the distinctions made in theory above might actually be used in practice . . .

Student A produced the following text as a telegram:

DAD BAD MARESBROOK HOSPITAL READING STOP BRING IMMEDIATELY YOURSELF MUM VERY NERVOUS STOP ROBERTA

The marking of this text will not involve any criticism of the handling of text–type or the handling of ellipsis which characterises the language of telegrams. This student, it can be seen, doesn't need to continue practising the writing of telegrams *per se*. However, work on semantics and grammar is seen to be necessary.
a) DAD BAD could be ambiguous – presumably the word should be 'sick/ill'
b) BRING . . . YOURSELF is simply the wrong phrase (semantic reference); *come* is the normal expression
c) NERVOUS has been applied incorrectly too, probably a mistranslation. The intended word should be 'worried/upset'

These three errors of meaning are quite important and need correcting with counter examples, and even short exercises.

d) BRING IMMEDIATELY YOURSELF is grammatically unacceptable even though it is *not* confusing. As far as the text is concerned this error does not cause incomprehension, nor indeed could it. However, unacceptable word order deserves to be pointed out to students even if the nature of the error is less serious than the three mentioned above.

Student B produced this text as a telegram:

```
SORRY TELL YOU THAT DAD VY ILL IN MARESBROOK
HOSPITAL WITH A SEVERE BOUT OF PLEURESY MOMENT
HE IN SORREL WING AND IS VY SERIOUSLY ILL MUM IS
EXTREMELY WORRIED UPSET
```

In terms of spelling, syntax, morphology, semantics and reference this text is perfectly acceptable. The marking of it will be concerned with the issue of appropriacy. Although this student has understood to a certain extent the need for ellipsis, he has failed to grasp what conventions govern ellipsis in telegrams, i.e. he has omitted or shortened the wrong things. Secondly, the style is not that appropriate for a telegram. The phrase 'sorry to tell you' even in a shortened form, is not one you would expect in a telegram, particularly not for this purpose. This student then will need to devote more time to writing telegrams although his linguistic and semantic abilities are quite adequate.

BUILDING UP YOUR OWN RESOURCES

There are three areas, models, practices, and exercise materials, where this may be a valuable thing for the teacher using these books to do. As already stated, a foreign student has very restricted access to model text-types on which to base his own writing. Files of authentic materials for the units in *Writing Tasks*, used as supplementary reading materials, could make this gap a little narrower. Although plenty of practices have been provided in the Student's Book and in the Teacher's Book, the teacher on the spot may be aware of more authentic contexts for writing than the author of this book can possibly be. The adding of practice materials, either from your local newspaper, magazines, etc. or derived from genuine and immediate student need (e.g. Student X really does want to request something from an English or American company) would be invaluable in giving even more authenticity to the use of *Writing Tasks*. It has already been suggested that the exercise materials offered in the Teacher's Book are the minimum that may be required. Banks of exercise materials built up over years of experience for dealing with every conceivable writing problem are perhaps what the practising teacher should be aiming for. This would make the model of classroom practice suggested on page 2 more feasible and attractive.

Section 1 Writing notes and memos

Introduction

This section is devoted to the writing of short messages from one person to another. It is the least permanent of all writing and once a note is read it is usually discarded. Notes and memos range from being fairly formal messages between fellow employees and colleagues to quick informal contact in families or between friends.

The usual rhetorical conventions associated with letters are largely absent in notes. A date may be included, or a time, but the only essentials are an addressee and a sender's name.

An important feature of the language of notes and memos is ellipsis; that is the reduction of the normal level of linguistic redundancy for reasons of space or time, without lessening effectiveness or obscuring meaning. The social laws governing the use of acceptable ellipsis need to be clearly grasped as well as the linguistic laws. In fact, in the writing of notes and memos the social rules are very relaxed – people can shorten or not, as they think best: it tends to be a question of taste (unlike the writing of telegrams where the more urgent consideration of cost operates). Exercises on ellipsis are included for Unit 3.1 on page 39 of the Teacher's Book.

1.1 Explanations

These sorts of notes are written to people when something of importance has happened since you last saw someone, or because someone needs information that you haven't given them before, and won't be able to give them directly. Note that in the two models there are no dates: in the first because the message is only relevant to the addressee at the moment of reading the note; and in the second because the addressee knows from his work context precisely when the note was written and when the writer expected him to read it.

It is impossible to predict the language of this sort of note since an explanation usually involves description of some sort. The referential language used in description is quite beyond prediction. And consequently no language notes are attached to this unit.

Extra practice

Write both of these notes:

A You work for an English-speaking boss, in your own country. The police have just phoned your office to tell you of an accident in your family and you must go to the hospital.

 Leave a note for your boss explaining why you won't be in the office when he returns from his meeting. Suggest when you will see him again.

B Your friend is taking some of your things back to your own country for you after a stay in Britain. You've left the things lying in your landlady's/flatmate's front porch for your friend to collect.

 Write a note to your landlady/flatmate explaining this.

1.1 Test 1

Do both A and B:

A You share a flat with a friend. A decorator has just called to start work on some of the rooms. Leave a note to your friend – who will return when you're out – explaining what is going on and why.

B You have been working in an office for a week as a fill-in. The usual person has now returned. Leave a note explaining anything they may need to know, e.g. who called? post? new office procedure?

1.1 Test 2

Do both A and B:

A Your friend has been looking for a warm sweater. You have just seen one in a shop. Write a note to your friend explaining where you saw it, cost, colours, and anything else of relevance.

B You bought a book in Britain and took it back to your country. Now you've discovered that there is something wrong with the book (blank pages? poor printing?). Your friend is going to Britain soon and will take the book back to the shop for you.

 Write a note to the bookshop explaining the situation, and saying what you want done about it.

1.2 Arrangements

This kind of note is written when arrangements have been made by the writer that somehow involve the addressee, arrangements either about meetings (times, places) or about activities and transactions. The writer may be making contact directly (as in the first model in Unit 1.2) or may be relaying an arrangement from a third person (fourth model).

Important language items are exponents for making arrangements (will do) and ellipsis (e.g. 'meet you there' or 'back soon'). Other important areas of language are references to time and place (e.g. 'at/around/by 5.45 pm; at/near/by the fountain;). Sometimes when writing formal notes making arrangements, it is useful to list each point by using numbers and letters.

Extra practice

Write all three notes:

A Your host family has agreed to put your friend up for a few nights but you have only just found out when he is coming and how long he'll be staying. Leave a note for your hosts about this.

B You are working in an office when the phone rings with this call for an English colleague:

Miss Robey? ... well, if she's not in I'll have to leave a message for her ... I'm flying in from Verona, Italy, tomorrow ... I'm Mr Silvano Terzi by the way ... with a colleague and we'd like to see the new samples ... there's quite a lot of interest here. The plane touches down at Heathrow about ten past ten ...

Leave a note for your colleague explaining this arrangement.

C You and your parents have decided to go to two of the following theatre performances with a friend and you have just bought the tickets. Leave a note at your friend's hotel explaining what the arrangements are.

Comedy Theatre	STEAMING by Nell Dunn	7.30	£2.50, £3.75, £5, £7
Donmar Warehouse	HAMLET by Shakespeare	7.15	£1.50, £2, £3
Her Majesty's	AMADEUS by Peter Shaffer	7.30	£2, £3, £4.50, £6.50, £8
St Martin's	THE MOUSETRAP Agatha Christie	8.00	£2.50, £4, £7.50
Victoria Palace	WINDY CITY (musical)	7.30	£3.25, £4.50, £6.35, £7.20

1.2 Test 1

Do both A and B:

A Write your friend a note saying where you will be on Saturday morning and afternoon – and where he/she can meet you.

B An electrician phones your British host while he is out. You answer the phone. Write a message to your host after this call:

Well, if Mr X isn't in, could you leave this message for him. Ron Fulton called – I can't come and start that big job tomorrow after all – I've got to finish a job in town . . . but I'll probably be O.K. for the day after . . . if there's any problem tell him to give me a buzz. Got that? . . . O.K. Cheers.

1.2 Test 2

Do both A and B:

A You live with an English girl. Her brother phones from London. Leave a message for her:

. . . yes, I'm Rob, her brother . . . look could you tell her . . . I've sort of just decided to um . . . pop over and see her . . . the early plane from Heathrow . . . I should get there by lunchtime . . . or just after . . . not sure how long I'll be staying . . . maybe a fortnight . . . O.K. if you could just tell her anyway . . . she knows I do things on impulse!

B You are going to lunch. Leave a clear note for your boss telling him of an arrangement you've made for him with a client tomorrow; remind him of two things he has to do this afternoon as well.

1.3 Instructions

Notes giving instructions are more likely to be necessary for people performing services or for work colleagues. For instructions given to friends or to people in the family the distinction between instruction notes and request notes becomes a little blurred. Such notes are written when people are not going to be available for oral instructions, when something has been forgotten or when people are in a hurry.

Instruction notes are commonly preceded by a simple request 'I'd be grateful if you could do the following things for me'. The convention of using numbers or letters to itemise instructions is useful in instruction notes.

The common and only essential language exponent is the use of the simple imperative form (Buy six foolscap . . . / Tell the milkman that . . .). The use of the 'please' makes an instruction note seem less severe. Ellipsis, particularly of the article is common; sometimes an instruction can be reduced to a single noun phrase where the context makes the instruction unambiguous (see the second model note, 'potatoes').

1.3   Test 1

Do both A and B:

A You've just moved into a flat in a British town and you want newspapers delivered. Write a note instructing the newsagents to deliver certain daily, weekly and monthly papers and magazines.

B An English friend is going to stay in your house when you are not there. Leave your friend a set of instructions about what to do if he/she falls ill about getting (a) a doctor, (b) to hospital, (c) medicine.

1.3   Test 2

Do both A and B:

A You are living in a flat in Britain and you're organising a party for a group of friends. Write a list of things you want from the local supermarket for your party.

B Two close friends are coming to stay with you for a week. Unfortunately you won't be at home when they arrive. Leave them a note on your door telling them:
i)   How to get in.
ii) How to contact you.
iii) How to make tea or coffee.

1.4   Inquiries and requests

Request notes are ubiquitous so there is little need to discuss their use.
   In terms of their form, they often consist of (i) a request of some sort (for action, for something, for permission) and (ii) a reason for the request or vice versa. Such notes may range from great informality to businesslike formality and this naturally affects the language used,

and to some extent the degree of ellipsis. The four models should illustrate this adequately.

The range of language exponents for making requests in notes is probably as wide as that used in personal or formal letters.

familiar/informal/direct: do this . . .
                              I want you to do this . . .
                              can you do . . .

informal/polite: could you / could I
                    would you
tentative: would you mind doing . . .
tentative/polite/   I wonder if . . .
   more formal: Would it be possible for me to . . . / for you to . . .
                    Would you be so kind as to . . .

Practice has been devised at two rough levels: informal and more formal.

Extra practice

Write one *formal* and one *informal* note:

FORMAL

A You have a certificate from an English Language Institute but the certificate hasn't been signed. A friend has offered to take the certificate back to the Institute for you. Write a formal note to the Institute explaining the situation and asking for the signature.

INFORMAL

B You are going out early in the morning and your British hostess will be out when you return. You want to know if it will be all right to invite a couple of friends round tomorrow evening. You will need to use the kitchen too. Write a suitable note to your hostess.

C A friend is going into town. Leave some money and a note in his room asking him to buy a couple of things for you – give details (price? where from? size?).

1.4   Test 1

Do both A and B:

A Your friend is going into town early tomorrow. Write a note asking him/her to get you a theatre ticket for a particular performance, and to find out the time of this performance and details of other productions.

B You have to make an important call to an English firm in Britain but don't trust your own English. Write to an English-speaking colleague asking him/her to make the call for you.

1.4   Test 2

Do both A and B:

A Your friend is going to London tomorrow. You want to go to London next week for two days.
   Leave a note asking him/her to book you a room in a hotel.
   Suggest:
   i)   Price range.
   ii)   Area.
   iii) How many nights.

B You want to go to the west coast of Scotland and you would like some information, maps and advice about the best time to go and the best way of getting there. There is a Scottish woman (Mrs J. Mackie) living near you but you don't actually know her. Write her a formal note of inquiry and request.

1.5   Apologies and explanations

Notes of apology are written in the following circumstances: when you have failed to do something; when you have made an error or mistake; when you can't do something that you promised or expected to do.

There may be four distinct sections to a note of apology even when very short: (i) a regretful opening (ii) something apologised for (iii) a reason for the failure or mistake (iv) a promise to remedy the situation. Not all notes will include all four items.

Language notes are given with the model (Student's Book page 20) but it should be said that many foreign students find it quite difficult to write notes of apology and more practices are available for this section. Students do not always hit the right tone, either because they fail to sound truly apologetic, or because they sound effusively insincere.

Extra practice 1

Write *two* notes:

A Your landlord asked you to feed the cat while he was out, but you gave the cat the wrong food. Apologise and offer an explanation.

B You had planned (vaguely) to go to a folk concert with a friend but now another friend has asked you out to something more interesting. Write a *tactful* note of apology and explanation.

C You haven't returned a cassette to an English colleague and you are just leaving the country. Send the cassette back via someone else with a suitable note attached.

Notes of apology are difficult to do well. Take some care with the *tone*.

Extra practice 2

Write *two* notes:

A You made arrangements with your teacher to have a class meeting in a restaurant. You now realise that you told your teacher the wrong day and time. Send him/her an apologetic note with the right information.

B You work with an English-speaking colleague. You have just realised that you were rather abrupt with this person this morning (you were in a hurry). Send a note of apology and explanation.

C You borrowed a battery-operated radio from a friend, but unfortunately left the radio on all night. Write an apologetic note to him/her, and offer to . . .

1.5   Test 1

Do both A and B:

A You promised an English colleague that you'd find out some information for him about local train services. You've completely forgotten. Write a note of apology and explanation to him/her.

B You've spilt coffee all over a book that you'd borrowed from a friend. Leave the book and a note of apology at his/her house or flat.

1.5   Test 2

Do both A and B:

A You have just backed your car rather carelessly into another car, which you happen to know is owned by an American woman. You have scratched the other car, but the driver is nowhere to be seen.
    Write an explanation and apology to the driver (to leave on her windscreen) and suggest an arrangement.

B With horror you have just realised that you have completely forgotten a shopping trip you were going to make with a friend to a nearby town today. Write a note to leave at his/her house: a note of apology and – if possible – explanation.

Section 2   Writing personal letters

Introduction

This section is about writing letters to friends, relations and acquaintances with whom we need to make personal contact for social or private reasons. With the advent of the telephone and the tape-recorder, some people feel that the 'art' of letter-writing has declined; what is certainly true is that there has been a decrease in the number of personal letters written; it could also be suggested that less time is devoted to expressive and anecdotal letter-writing, that people write less for the pure pleasure of writing than for transactional reasons.

All literate cultures develop conventions of varying degrees of strictness to govern the writing of letters. In English, these conventions concern the position and layout of the contents in respect of the writer's address, the date, content and salutation; convention also governs the forms used for address, date and salutation. Despite these conventions, English native-speakers often adopt quite idiosyncratic styles in personal letters, and the foreign writer of personal letters need not be unduly worried about breaking the 'laws' of letter-writing.

With the exception of the items mentioned in the preceding paragraph (see Section 2 Introduction in the Student's Book, page 22) linguistic items will be specific to particular units. The linguistic requirements for some units are easy to anticipate (in letters of apology or thank-you letters, for instance); in other units, however, it would be fatuous to make any linguistic suggestions (e.g. Unit 2.9).

It must be said that although each unit in Section 2 is presented as a viable letter type, it is quite possible for a single letter to combine a number of the implied functions in various units together in one text; for example, one may write a thank-you letter which also includes a whole section on the making of arrangements for some future event. It is also quite possible, and perhaps quite likely, that personal letters will include whole paragraphs of text that belong more properly to other sections in this book such as writing descriptions, reporting experiences, or expressing opinions.

2.1 Invitations

This sort of letter is an invitation to action of some sort: to visit a place, to attend an event, to make a contribution and so on. Occasionally in English an invitation takes a particular form, as in party and wedding invitations; normally, however, letters of invitation are not unnecessarily formal in their writing.

The language necessary to write these letters covers three areas:

i)   making invitations: direct, tentative and more formal (see model in the Student's Book) invitations can also be made in the form of suggestions.

ii) circumstantial description: describing actions and states in the present, up to the present and in the future.

iii) reason-giving: so, because, since etc. conjuncts: consequently, therefore.

Writers of invitation letters frequently append a final sentence of hope or expectation such as 'I (do) hope you can (you'll be able to) come / make it.'

2.1   Test 1

A friend is making a short business trip to your country. He'll be staying in a hotel, but would perhaps appreciate being shown round. Write a letter inviting him to go to various places with you, and do things which might interest him in your town/country.

2.1   Test 2

You are getting married soon. Write a letter inviting a very old and close friend to your wedding. Give a few details in the letter.

2.2   Requests and inquiries

Letters in which people ask for a favour or some information are so common that no comment on their use is necessary. In terms of content, making requests is normally accompanied by other language acts such as descriptions of circumstances and explanations for requests. There are no special conventions in the writing of request letters and 'signing off' phrases such as 'thanking you in advance' are certainly not necessary and may even be regarded as over-insistent by some people.

The language exponents used in request letters vary according to two factors: the intimacy of the relationship between writer and addressee on the one hand, and the delicacy or difficulty of the request task on the other.

Relationship	Language	Task
polite and friendly ↓	Could you/would you ... ?	simple ↓

polite and more
formal
↓
	Would you mind doing ... ?
	Would/could you possibly ... ?
	Would it be possible for you
	   to ... ?
	I wonder if you could/would ... ?
	Is there any chance of
	   | you/your | doing ... ?
	   | me/my |
		difficult or
		delicate
		↓

very polite	Would you be
	   | so kind as to ... ?
	   | kind enough to ... ?	

Students should receive clear guidance on this when their work is marked.

Extra practice 1

Write *one* letter of request and *one* of inquiry:

REQUEST

A While you were in England an acquaintance made a delicious chocolate cake. Write and ask her/him for the recipe. Say why you want to make it.

INQUIRY

B You've just taken up the guitar, and you want to know the best simple music to start with. A friend of a colleague might be able to tell you, but you have only met him once before. Write to him to inquire.

Extra practice 2

Write both A and B:

REQUEST

A You are a dressmaker or furniture-maker. A friend asked you to make a winter coat or a table. You want to start it now but you haven't the faintest idea what sort of coat or table he or she wants (size? materials? style?). Write a letter requesting instructions for the making of this coat or table.

INQUIRY

B You haven't been to Britain for a number of years, and you need to find out about the cost of living. Write to an old friend asking for information about cost of transport, hotels, food, clothes and alcohol – be specific in *some* of your inquiries.

2.2   Test 1

A short while ago you spent three months in Britain on an English language course. Write a letter to your British hosts *or* to your course tutor (a) inquiring about the local employment situation in the area of Britain you were staying in – especially in the kind of work you want to do and (b) requesting information about work permits.

2.2   Test 2

You met a British girl in your country who works at the British Council Office. You want to know about borrowing music records from the Council and also where you can order records directly from Britain.

2.3   Acceptances and refusals

Invitations or offers made verbally in person or on the phone, or by letter or formal invitation need to be responded to: we can either refuse or accept them. First, you need to thank the addressee for his or her invitation or offer before accepting or refusing. When refusing, it is normal to express regret at having to refuse, and it is seen as impolite not to give a reason for turning down the offer or invitation. An alternative date or activity is often suggested.

As suggested in the language notes in the Student's Book (page 29) there are simple formal ways of phrasing an actual refusal.

Since this sort of letter usually refers to aspects of the future, it may be important for students to be able to write about plans, ambitions, fears, hopes and expectations in the future.

2.3 Test 1

Write *two* letters for the situation:
A friend is going to tour Yugoslavia during July and has written to ask if you would like to go with him or her.
1 A letter of acceptance, expressing your pleasure.
2 A letter of refusal: polite, firm and offering an explanation for refusal.

2.3 Test 2

Write *two* letters for the situation:
This is part of a letter from someone who was on a cruise with you:
'... so we've decided to have a reunion party in Austria on the 20th July. We're hoping you can come. ...'
1 A letter of acceptance, expressing your pleasure.
2 A letter of refusal: polite, firm, and offering an explanation for your refusal.

2.4 Arrangements

Letters discussing arrangements may be written about the plans or arrangements of the writer himself or on behalf of someone else. The arrangements may concern holidays, trips or attendance at events and meetings; they may deal with practical contingencies such as money matters or personal requirements.

Important language points have been indicated on page 31 of the Student's Book:
– describing personal arrangements for the future;
– describing timetabled events for the future;
– reporting and expressing plans and ambitions;
– expressing expectations and anticipations.

Other notional language will also be needed:

i) exact time reference: on a day
at a clock time
in a week/month/year
at the end of . . . / beginning of . . .
in the middle of . . .

ii) approximate time reference: at about / sometime in . . .
three-thirty-ish . . .

iii) future time in reference to present: tomorrow
two weeks from now
in two weeks' time
the day after tomorrow

iv) place reference: at/in/by/near

Extra practice

Write *one* letter:

A You and your brother or sister are going to stay with a family in Britain while you both study/work. Write to your host and hostess discussing arrangements you need to make for:
your arrival
sleeping arrangements
meals (time / special diet?)
clothes-washing
anything else relevant

B You've arranged to spend a week with a British friend in his or her home town. Write a letter suggesting a rough timetable for your week. (Football matches take place on Saturday afternoons; you want to do some shopping at Marks and Spencers; you are very keen to hear some jazz; there's an exhibition of pottery in the town.)

2.4 Test 1

This is your diary for a weekend in London:

Friday night	Turkish restaurant with Turkish friend
Saturday	
	9-11 Visit Portobello Road market
	3-5 Watch football match (Chelsea)
	9-? French film (Truffaut)
Sunday	
	1-3 Friend for lunch
	5 Start journey back

You want to fit in a meeting with a friend sometime over the weekend. Write a letter explaining your present arrangements and suggesting possible meeting times.

2.4 Test 2

A friend wrote to you a few days ago about coming to see you for a week in the Easter holidays. In her letter she wanted to do some of the following things:
a) visit a local pottery
b) see a local football match
c) eat out somewhere
d) visit a friend of hers who lives near you
Write a letter back to her, suggesting some arrangements to do all or some of these things during her week with you (from Sunday, 13th April to Saturday, 19th April); you might like to add one or two of your own suggestions to the arrangements.

2.5 Apologies and explanations

Letters of apology are written in the following circumstances: when you have failed to do something expected of you at some time in the past (e.g. you promised to send someone a book but you have failed to do so); when you have made a mistake of some sort (e.g. you've booked a friend into the wrong hotel in your country); when you are unable to do something expected of you or promised by you (e.g. you cannot, after all, have your friend to stay at Easter).

To write successful letters of apology, writers need to be able to do the following things:

i) *express regretful apology*
   informal: I feel awful about . . .
               I'm (terribly/very) sorry about . . .
   more formal: I (do) apologise . . . for . . .
                  I sincerely apologise . . .
                  Please accept my (sincere) apologies for . . .

ii) *offer reasons and explanations for the failure or mistake*
    introduction: Sadly, . . .
                    Unfortunately, I . . .

iii) *make promises to remedy*   I promise | that . . .
                                            | I'll . . .
     express hopes for future (improvements) I hope to . . .
                                      I assure you that . . .

iv) *express sympathy for inconvenience caused*
    I realise how upset/difficult . . .
    I do hope it didn't . . .

Although the student needs to be able to express the things suggested above, the success of a letter of apology depends upon the tact and delicacy with which the writer deals with a difficult situation. The classroom teacher will need to use his own sensitivity to tone and context in order to mark such work. The same caveats are offered here as have been offered in the notes to Unit 1.5.

Extra practice 1

Write *one* of the following letters:

A You and a friend used the country cottage of a friend of yours for the weekend. Unfortunately, you woke up much later than you had intended on the Monday morning and had to leave in a great hurry. You left the cottage in a somewhat messy condition.
   Write a letter of apology to your friend about this, and explain how it came to happen.

B You were going to help a British teacher in your country organise an international evening on the Saturday after next. For personal reasons you will now be unable to be there. You feel you are letting the teacher down so write an apologetic letter explaining the situation.

Extra practice 2

Write *one* of the following letters:

A You have been involved with a group of Americans visiting your country for two weeks and you've got to know them quite well. On the night before they leave for home they intend to hold a party (they are leaving at 5 the next morning!). Naturally, they have invited you.

   On the night of the party you suddenly find that you are unable to go. You won't see them again since they are leaving early the following morning. Write a letter to them (or the group leader) apologising for your failure to go to the party.

B You receive a letter from a friend with this section in it:

> I think Rosie was quite upset over her visit to you. She said that you were almost rude to her, and seemed distinctly uninterested in her new job. This sounds very unlike you

You know the writer is probably right, but on that particular day you had a lot of family and work pressures, and also a bad headache. Write a letter apologising to Rosie.

2.5   Test 1

When you return to your own country, you find you've got your hostess's hair-dryer in your luggage, and two tickets to a play in Oxford! Write a letter of apology and explanation.

2.5   Test 2

You are a fairly good amateur weaver. You make carpets, rugs, wall-hangings, and cushion-covers. While visiting you recently, a Scottish friend asked you to make a wall-hanging for her. You agreed, but unfortunately you have found the pattern you agreed on impossible to weave, and there are one or two other problems as well. Write a letter apologising for this.

2.6   Congratulations and commiserations

This kind of text may exist in its own right or form part of a larger personal letter. We express feelings of pleasure and shared excitement when people are the recipients of life's bounties. In times of sadness, loss, failure or tragedy we express appropriate sympathy.

There is little to say about the textual organisation of such letters apart from suggesting that two things are required: a reference to the event or issue which is the cause of the letter and then an expression, extended or brief, of congratulation or commiseration. In offering commiseration, however, a very brief letter might seem cold and unfeeling; we might also wish to offer help.

It is impossible and undesirable to offer definite help on the expressions of these emotions in English because individuals develop and use their own style of expression, even in foreign languages. Some suggestions have been made in the language notes section of the Student's Book (page 35); the teacher's responsibility will be to evaluate the tone of such writing and encourage sincerity and directness.

Extra practice 1

Write to *one* of the following people:

A   An acquaintance who has just passed his or her final university exams in Law, or as a doctor, engineer, or accountant.

B   A person who you knew quite well when you were in Britain, who has just had her fourth baby – all girls!

Now write to *one* of these people:

C   An old friend who has just lost his job and is rather depressed. Don't be too hearty.

D   A friend you used to know in your own country, who is now rather upset because a close friend has just committed suicide.

Extra practice 2

Write a letter to *one* of the following people:

A A friend whose house or flat has just burned down in a fire which destroyed most of his or her possessions.

B An 18-year-old acquaintance whose parents are going through a painful, unpleasant divorce.

Write *one* of the following letters:

C To an acquaintance of yours who at the age of 64 has just acquired a pilot's licence!

D To a friend who is a potter and who has recently become very successful. You saw a programme about her on local TV recently.

2.6 Test 1

Do both A and B:

A Someone you know quite well, of the same sex as you, has just got married for the second time (divorced the first time). Write and congratulate this person.

B A friend of yours wants to become a nurse, but has just failed some important exams. Write and commiserate with her.

2.6 Test 2

Do both A and B:

A A friend of yours has just won a story-writing competition, with a prize of £1,000. Write, with surprise and pleasure, to congratulate him or her.

B A friend of yours hasn't got on well with her parents for a long while – now, after a long series of arguments and unpleasant scenes, she's moved out into her own flat. Write a letter of sympathy and commiseration about this unfortunate break with her parents.

2.7 Thank-you letters

The reasons for and uses of thank-you letters need no comment.
When they exist in their own right they are usually very short, simple
and direct; over-flowery thank-you letters may well invite the
accusation of being insincere.

   The contents of a thank-you letter include the following:
i)   thanking (I'm very grateful to you . . .)
ii) describing pretext (. . . for making my stay in Edinburgh so
                          pleasant and for . . .)
iii) expressing pleasure (I enjoyed myself enormously . . .)
Simple suggestions about language have been made in the language
notes section in the Student's Book (page 39).

2.7   Test 1

While you were in England, you became acutely depressed. A friend
of the same age was very understanding and sympathetic, and spent a
lot of time trying to cheer you up and sort you out. Write a thank-you
letter to this person.

2.7   Test 2

A few weeks ago, when you were in Great Britain on a holiday, you
asked a friend if she could get two books for you that you hadn't been
able to obtain from a bookshop. Today a parcel arrived from Britain
with both books, and a third! Write an appropriate thank-you letter
to your friend for the trouble and expense she has gone to for you.

2.8   Expressing positive and negative emotions

Although the practices in this unit have been organised to suggest that
the unit embraces a text-type complete in itself, expressing positive
and negative emotions occurs in any sort of personal letter-writing,
and thus nothing very useful can be suggested about the 'form' of
such letters. When expressing emotions we usually relate them to
external things or events.

   The expression of emotion is a very large area indeed and it is
impossible to suggest even a partial language inventory. However, the

33

Council of Europe's Threshold Level offers some help in its content specification *Language functions with exponents*, Section 3: 'Expressing and finding out emotional attitudes'. Two other publications for oral work, but which may be useful here are *Choose Your English* (BBC 1970) and *Feelings* (CUP 1980). In the latter, the authors suggest that the book can be used in the area of informal composition (i.e. personal letter-writing).

The following emotions are those that foreign writers may most commonly wish to learn to express:

anger, irritation, depression, worry and anxiety, disappointment, regret,

and

excitement, anticipation, enthusiasm, delight, admiration, desire, hope, relief, surprise, affection and love.

A warning note: setting up contextualised practices for this unit carries the inevitable danger of encouraging insincere writing from simulated rather than real emotion.

Extra practice 1

Write *two* letters, one expressing positive emotions and one negative emotions:

POSITIVE

A   You've just either (i) seen a fascinating exhibition of paintings, or (ii) been to a marvellous theatre performance. Write to a friend expressing your enthusiasm, and delight with your experience.

B   You've just recovered from a long and serious illness; it's spring; you've also just rediscovered an old friend. Write a happy letter to another good friend, expressing what you feel at the moment.

NEGATIVE

C   You're in England: the weather is absolutely awful; you're finding it very difficult to live in what seems an unfriendly place. Write a letter to a friend in London, expressing how miserable you feel.

D   You've failed to get two jobs you applied for. You were fairly certain that you'd get one of them so you're very disappointed. Write a letter to a friend.

Write *two* letters, one expressing positive emotions, one negative emotions:

POSITIVE

A Write a very positive, happy letter to a friend expressing your happiness and delight with your new job in a new town and with your new social life there.

B In about a week's time you are going to do one or more of the things listed below:
   i)   a journey in South America
   ii)   a new job
   iii) start living with your boy/girl friend
   iv)   get married
   Write a letter of hope, optimism, and anticipation to a close friend.

NEGATIVE

C You are very angry and irritated with the language course you are attending in Britain. Write an appropriate letter to the friend in your own country who recommended it.

D After a very happy stay in a foreign country, you've returned to your home town. You are very depressed – by your job, by the place you live in, and particularly by the people you work with. Write a letter to a close friend, expressing just how you feel about your life at the moment.

2.9   General personal letters

Most personal letters seem to be a mixture of things, descriptions, comments, requests, etc., containing everything we need to say in order to retain contact with a friend, a member of our family, or an acquaintance. These letters may have many functions, including all those suggested in the eight previous units in this section: inviting, requesting, inquiring, arranging, apologising, thanking, refusing and accepting offers and invitations, expressing positive and negative emotions. Personal letters are also full of description and reporting – thus practice in Sections 4 and 5 will be useful for successful writing in this unit.

The practices for this unit are inevitably simulated, even if genuinely contextualised. However, there may be ways of making authentic writing the practice for this unit – for example, by writing letters to penfriends.

Two topic areas of language it may be useful to suggest for such letters are *health* and *weather*.

Extra practice 1

Write a chatty letter to a British friend who is living in your country. Write about the following things:
a) Ask in detail for your friend's impressions of your country.
b) The 'food' you're eating, and comment on what your friend said about food in your country in his or her last letter.
c) Describe an odd/funny/disturbing incident that happened to you in town the other day.
d) Comment on English Sundays.

Extra practice 2

Write a chatty letter to a friend in London where you were living until about three months ago. Do the following things:
a) Write about the people you're staying with and describe something (an incident) that happened in the family.
b) Compare things in this town to things in your home town, and comment.
c) Say something about English breakfasts.
d) Comment upon the new job your friend has found.
e) You've heard about an accident that happened to a mutual friend. You know your friend knows more about the accident. Ask about it.

2.9 Test 1

Write a letter to an English friend who lives in another British town – in fact, you used to live in this town too.
a) Write about the differences between the two towns (atmosphere/ feeling).
b) Comment on new people you've met.
c) Describe an argument you got into in a restaurant.
d) Say how long your stay is going to be and discuss future plans.
e) Comment on a book you've just read or a film you've just seen.
f) End the letter.

2.9   Test 2

The extract below is part of a letter from a British friend. With the
help of the notes added to the letter, write a reply, commenting on
what he says and answering the questions in it.

Christmas

the Christmas period is just over. I used to think *here*
Christmas in this country was just an excuse to eat and drink
too much - I now think it's an excuse to lie supine in front
of a TV set; everyone I went to see seemed to be glued to the
box. Some people were just passive; others apologetic but
still passive. What's it like in your country - I can't
believe it's like that there? I've read quite a lot during
the holiday and one novel I read was Fontane's 'Effi Briest'.
I didn't know there were any novels in 19th-Century Germany,
but this one is splendid. I don't know whether the trans-
lation has altered the style but it's a very cryptic under-
stated style. I don't know whether you've read it or not.
What have you been reading lately? Anything you can
recommend? *Yes*

When you last wrote you were just going off to see your old
infants' school teacher; do tell me what that was like.
Funnily enough, I bumped into my old French teacher last
week. We used to think she was an absolute dragon at school.
It's funny how quiet and pleasant she seemed now. We even
talked about the weather, like talking to your next door *Weather*
neighbour. Actually, the weather is almost worth talking
about; it's the middle of the winter and it's the weather for
May, people are walking around with just pullovers and
jumpers on! I don't suppose it's like that where you are?!

Mum
I had a Christmas card from your parents. I felt very *and Dad*
touched that they remembered me. Do tell me how they both
are now that they've retired. I always wonder how busy
people like they seemed to be manage to fill the day when
they give up work and

Section 3 Writing telegrams, personal ads and instructions

Introduction

The grouping together of these three units into one section is fairly arbitrary on any functional grounds. What can perhaps be said is that the three sorts of writing are instrumental in particular actions – buying, selling, moving, doing, and as such we may regard this section as the practice of written communication in the service of effective action.

Telegrams are a form of letter in a highly compressed state. Personal advertisements are written to enable people to contact a general readership for a specific purpose (the pursuit or offer of specific goods or services, for example). Instructions are written to either a specific or a general readership to facilitate the carrying out of actions such as cooking or the operation of equipment.

The written conventions differ in the three units too. Telegrams are simply elliptical messages. Small ads require the use of a special set of terminologies and associated abbreviations. Instructions use numerical, alphabetical and visual aids.

However, all the units in this section share one important linguistic feature: that of ellipsis (either because words in themselves cost money or because there is a premium on space). Small ads and telegrams both demand the use of elliptical devices in the desire to reduce cost. Instructions use ellipsis in the interests of conciseness and clarity. The exercises for Unit 3.1 on page 39 of this book will give the student some practice in abbreviating normal English to elliptical versions, if this should be necessary before tackling all these units.

3.1 Writing telegrams and telexes

Few people would write a telegram if they had the time to write a letter. The emphasis upon rapid delivery of a message and the consequent effect upon the cost of the transmission affects the form that the telegram or telex traditionally takes, as well as its uses. Telegrams and telexes are used to transmit, at speed, instructions, good and bad news, urgent information, and celebratory greetings and messages of affection, sympathy, and congratulation. A telegram or telex usually takes the form of a continuous and highly elliptical text, which involves the deletion of most articles and determiners, many pronouns and possessive indications, and the auxiliary parts of verbs. Students who need to practise elliptical writing should do the exercises on page 39 of this book.

3.1 Exercises

The exercises below are designed to help you shorten normal English sentences.

1 UNDERSTANDING ELLIPTICAL WRITING

In this section the sentences are already short. Write these out in full English sentences to show that you understand what has been left out.
a) Get me half pound potatoes, two lemons.
b) Leaving London immediately; back Monday.
c) Jack gone! Where?
d) Bought camera – takes good pics!
e) Father sick – can't make wedding.

2 TAKING WORDS OUT

Make the sentences below as short as you can *without losing any of the meaning* – be careful about this!

Examples: (I)'ll bring (the) tickets later in (the) evening.
           Will bring tickets later in evening.

a) It's raining here at the moment.
b) Mary is unable to come on Saturday.
c) We're having lovely weather.
d) How did you get on with my sister?
e) The key is at home on the table by the window.
f) Sue is not going to Italy because she's fallen in love with an Austrian boy.
g) Get all the money that you need from Harry.
h) Why didn't Joe come? Please could you explain this.
i) My sister won't be returning yet; perhaps in a fortnight's time.
j) Richard loves me so we're getting married soon.

3 REPHRASING

Sometimes you can make a text shorter by using different words. Do this with the texts below:
a) Harry's wife, children and grandmother didn't turn up on time.
b) Every single person here is having a jolly good time.
c) He drinks beer, wine and spirits in great quantities.

Writing telegrams, personal ads and instructions

Extra practice

Write four of the following telegrams:

A To a friend on holiday in Scotland – his or her sister has just arrived from Canada.

B To a Japanese company in Osaka – flight problems might cause you to arrive late for your business meeting . . .

C The woman you stayed with in Britain has just come out of hospital – send a suitable telegram.

D An American friend has asked you to find a record on sale in your country. You can't get it. Send a telegram to him or her with another suggestion as well.

E You have fallen crazily in love and this means that you now need to change some arrangements you had made to meet an English friend.

F You and a friend are on holiday in Mexico. Your friend is ill – inform his or her sister by telegram.

3.1 Test 1

Write three telegrams for the following occasions:

A You were going to meet a friend in the capital of your country. Now you must change your plans.

B You are in Wales on holiday. There have been severe storms and flooding, and consequent loss of life. Reassure your British hosts about your safety, whereabouts, and mood.

C You are back in your own country. An acquaintance asked you to send him/her a book absolutely immediately. You can't get it. Suggestions?

Write three telegrams for the following occasions:

A A friend has just had her third baby.

B Your friend asked for a cassette of folk music from your country –
   but there are a lot of cassettes – ask him or her to be more specific.

C You have found some information about flight times to and from
   your city or nearest airport to London. Send this information to
   your friend (this telegram may need to be longer but should still be
   concise).

3.2   Writing personal ads

Foreign users of English will not want or need to write personal
advertisements unless they have ready access to the (local) British
press, or a local press in English. Generally speaking then, the writing
of small ads will only be valuable for students living or intending to
live in English-speaking countries. They are used for selling and
buying goods and services, advertising needs or opportunities, or
making general announcements.

   Like telegrams, small ads cost money – the lengthier the
advertisement, the more costly the exercise. Thus the art of writing
small ads is that of compressing the message by the use of
abbreviations, figures and numbers, and grammatical ellipsis into the
smallest space possible. The use of abbreviations has come to be
specific to the topic of the ad: for example, accommodation adverts
have their own language (e.g. rec. inc., pw, H & C, CH etc.).

   Ellipsis can be severe, removing all articles and generally doing
without a verb phrase.

3.2 Test 1

Write all three small ads:

A You want to buy/sell a radio. Give details or requirements.

B You want to stay for a time in the South-West with an English family. Give details.

C You need work, sometime in the future, in a hotel in England. Give precise details (requirements and qualifications).

3.2 Test 2

Write all three small ads:

A You bought an umbrella during your stay in Britain. Now you want to sell it (age? price? colour?).

B You've been staying with an English family but now you want to move out and rent a house (rent £? size? location? how long for?).

C You're in Britain on a rather long business trip. You need a private English teacher (how often? salary range?).

3.3 Writing instructions

Apart from instructions used in the study or work fields of technology and business, the kinds of instructions that a foreign user of English may be called upon to use are relatively easily identified. They are the giving of directions, instructions for the preparation of food and drink, instructions concerning the operation of simple household equipment, and procedures used to get something done officially.

The rhetorical features found in written instructions involve the use of a certain amount of ellipsis (particularly of the article); the use of numbers, letters, and discrete paragraphs for organising and sequencing instructions; and the use of aids such as labelled diagrams, maps, and pictures.

Sets of instructions may contain certain distinct semantic features: instructions (including warnings, advice, prohibitions), descriptions of means or methods, statements of reasons or purpose, and descriptions of likely outcomes. The language notes on page 53 of the Student's Book offer advice on the language exponents involved. The exercises that follow practise these and other language points associated with writing instructions.

3.3 Exercises

1 EXPRESSING PURPOSE

In the following sentences about gardening use *in order to* or *to* to explain the purpose of following a particular instruction:

example: Prune fruit trees ...
Prune fruit trees in order to allow sunlight into the centre of the tree.

a) Water young plants ...
b) Add fertilisers ...
c) ..., mow the grass regularly.
d) Take off dead flower-heads ...

2 EXPRESSING METHOD

In the following sentences about making things with tools use:
by + VERB-ing (... by cutting along the line ...)
or by means of + NOUN (... by means of a spirit-level)
by using a + NOUN (... by using a calculator)
with a + NOUN

a) Cut the wood in half by ...   (saw)
b) Measure the wood ...   (ruler)
c) Tighten the screws ...   (screwdriver)
d) Make holes in the wood ...   (drill)
e) Remove the rough edges ...   (plane)
f) Polish the finished object ...   (bees wax)
g) Attach handles ...   (glue and screws)

3   SEQUENCING INSTRUCTIONS

Sometimes it is useful to add words to instructions that show the
order in which things are done.

example: Teeth-brushing   First, put toothpaste on the brush.
                           Then, brush teeth vigorously from side to side.
                           At the same time, ensure that the insides
                             of the teeth are thoroughly cleaned.
                           Finally, rinse toothpaste and food debris
                             out of the mouth.

In the next two exercises use the expressions: First/Then/Next/After
that/At the same time/Finally.

a) Put these instructions about washing hair in order, and add the
    right sequencing words:
    – rinse hair in clean water / rub hair dry with a towel / apply
      shampoo / wet hair thoroughly / undo shampoo bottle / comb
      hair / rub in shampoo.

b) Now write a sequence of instructions for making toast, using these
    ideas in the order here:
    – switch on grill
    – slice bread
    – place ...
    – brown both sides
    – switch off ...
    – butter

4   WORDS AND PHRASES

Check the meaning of these words: switch / handle / button / knob /
                                   dial / pedal / indicator / lever

A Put one word from above into each sentence:

   a) The .... said that the petrol tank was empty.

   b) You carry a radio by its ....

   c) Push the .... to call the tutor.

   d) There are three light .... in the room.

   e) He tried all the .... at the back of the TV set.

   f) There are two kinds of brake in a car: one of them works

       when you use a .... , the other one when you

       push down a ....

B Complete the following sentences:

a) When you make a radio louder you turn ....

b) When you don't want the radio on you switch ....

c) When you want to boil milk you put ....

d) When you want cigarettes from a machine you push ....

Extra practice

Write out three of the four sets of instructions:

A *Procedures*
Write out a clear set of instructions describing the best way to rent a flat or house in your country.

B *Recipe*
Write out a recipe for cooking rice or potatoes with a method or style used in your own country – so that friends can get more variety into their cooking.

C *Directions*
With the help of a simple sketchmap, if necessary, write out a set of directions from the airport (or station) in your town to your home.

D *Technical instructions*
Using a diagram if necessary (and it probably is!) explain, in a set of instructions, how your record-player is operated so that a friend can use it while you are away.

3.3 Test 1

Do both A and B:

A Leave precise instructions, with a diagram, for a friend, explaining how to use the cooker in your home.
or
Write out clear instructions for the proper cooking and serving of spaghetti.

B With the help of a labelled map, give clear directions to help someone get from the town centre to your home.

Writing telegrams, personal ads and instructions

3.3 Test 2

Do both A and B:

A A friend is about to borrow your camera, calculator or cassette player. When you give it to him or her, also leave a set of clear operating instructions.

B An English-speaking friend is coming to stay in your country. He wants to know how to use the public telephone system for *ordinary calls* and *emergency calls*. Write out a set of clear instructions for this person.

Section 4   Writing descriptions

Introduction

In this section (and in the following section on reporting), the relation between the function of writing, in this case describing, and particular text-types cannot be specified as directly as in most of the units in previous sections. Descriptions may form text-types of their own, as they do frequently in advertising copy, or poetry, or they may occur within the confines of other text-types including personal letters, small ads, reports, and more professional writing such as brochures. It is likely that foreign students and users of English will be writing description in the latter category.

Similarly, the rhetorical conventions that govern the writing of descriptions proceed not from the descriptions themselves but from the use to which they are put, and the context in which they are found. Thus the description of a transistor radio will alter in terms of the textual conventions with which it is written according to whether it is to be advertised in a small ad, written about to a friend, or complained about to a radio dealer.

The language required for descriptions is virtually the whole of the propositional language available in English. To attempt a summary in this introduction would be somewhat absurd. However, it can be said that four of the units deal with *stative* description (of people, places, objects, landscape); two with *universalistic* description (of habits and conditions and processes); one unit deals with *dynamic* description (of present scenes and activities). Consequently particular units will obviously require specific areas of propositional language, and particular language uses (e.g. tense, aspect, modality).

All seven units are about describing life as it *is*.

4.1   Describing people

The need to describe people occurs fairly often, although most writers of language do not usually need to write long descriptions to achieve their purpose. The informal description of other people or even of oneself is common in personal letters. The description of self occurs in job applications; the writing of reports and essays may involve the description of other people.

The following areas may all form part of personal description:

i) physical attributes (hair, eyes, complexion, facial shape, other facial features, build, height, gait, gesture, dress – and related descriptive notions: size, colour, style, decoration)

ii) emotional, (e.g. warm, aloof, nervous ...)
intellectual (e.g. clever, mediocre, perceptive ...)
and moral (e.g. trustworthy, greedy ...)
attributes

iii) habitual attributes (behavioural and emotional habits, opinions, gesture and expression)

4.1   Exercises 1

1   HAIR, EYES, COMPLEXION

Place the following words into three separate lists: *Hair, Eyes, Complexion.* Some of the words will go into two or even three of the lists.

pale / fair / auburn / green / hazel / nut-brown / sallow / ruddy / dark / ginger / rosy / mousy / dull / curly / almond-shaped / bloodshot / lank / frizzy / spotty / pasty / bright / bobbed / large / long

Now write an X beside the words which you think are negative!

2   GENERAL PHYSICAL DESCRIPTIONS

a) Put these words into the spaces below:

fingers / broad / jaw / brown / faced / wavy / set / blue / legs

The round- .... man went through the door on his

short, stumpy .... His long .... hair

was an extraordinary reddy-..................... colour. His eyes

were rather deep-..................... and light-..................... .

How square and set his .... was! How ....

his shoulders! Only his long, delicate, restless ....

modified this impression of determination.

b) Find a good word to put in the spaces in this passage:

The police are looking for a ....-haired girl with

grey-green .... Her .... and

.... are .... like her hair. She is rather

pale in .... ; the face is .... She is very

.... , almost thin, and about 5 foot 3 inches

.... She has thin .... and a snub

....

3 DRESS

Put these items of clothing into four lists (women's clothes: indoor/ outdoor; men's clothes: indoor/outdoor):

a suit / a trouser-suit / a duffle-coat / a dinner jacket / a scarf / tights / a rollneck / a sweater / wellingtons / a waistcoat / cords / overalls

Match these words describing *how* people dress with the people in the list below:

neatly / elegantly / casually / scruffily / scantily / formally

(a) the Queen   (b) sunbathers   (c) a hitchhiker   (d) a wine-waiter
(e) a bank manager   (f) a bank manager at home

4 COMPLIMENTS AND INSULTS

Put a tick beside the expressions that you think are complimentary and a cross next to those you think are somewhat insulting:

The woman: is skinny
            is petite
            is slim
            is plump
            slouches
            has full lips

The man: is short and squat
          has B.O.
          strides about
          is distinguished-looking

Exercises 2

These exercises are concerned with the language that describes character and habits in people.

1   QUALITIES OF MIND

Put these words into three lists (*positive, negative, neutral*) and then try to find words or phrases which mean the opposite of each word given:

bright / simple-minded / silly / brilliant / sane / imaginative / witty / brainy / naive

2   MORAL QUALITIES

Put the following words into two lists (*Positive moral qualities* and *Negative moral qualities*):

sincere / unselfish / mean / callous / patient / insensitive / affectionate / devious / fair / trusting / vain / cruel

Now use the words from the list above to complete the following sentences:

a) Although she was tired and bored, her .... neighbour went on talking.

b) An .... person is one who thinks of others as well as himself, and often before himself.

c) I never know what he's up to! He's very ....

d) He's rather .... ; I don't think I've ever seen him buy anybody a drink.

e) He was an .... father, and loved being with his family even more than at his desk.

f) To ignore the problems of the unemployed would be a very .... policy.

g) 'I found the British ridiculously .... in the matter of queueing ... waiting for hours at a time without complaint for non-existent buses and trains.'

3   OTHER QUALITIES

Pick out six of the following words and describe people in your family
with them – giving an exammle each time to justify your description.

example: My brother is exceptionally *versatile*: a fine scientist, a
colourful weaver, a competent musician, a good cook, and
a gardener with a sure touch.

ambitious / determined / weak / indolent / self-confident / cynical /
uncomplicated / sceptical / naive / credulous / self-reliant / nervous /
irritable / unflappable / extravagant / reserved / blunt / charming /
misanthropic / weird / sentimental / emotional / passionate /
conservative / sanctimonious / pompous / dependent / versatile

4   FACIAL EXPRESSION

smile / frown / grin / grimace / scowl / laugh / pout / sulk

a) When angry, he ....

b) Bad jokes make me ....

c) Worry makes you ....

d) Children often .... and ....

e) Happy schoolboys often ....

Extra practice

In writing your descriptions concentrate upon all of the following
things:

Physical appearance:	face	Character:	facial and bodily
	body and figure		expressions
	gait and posture		habits
	typical clothes		abilities
			moods
			general character

Do both A *and* B:

A Describe a foreign person you've met.

B Describe a person you work or study with.

4.1   Test 1

Describe in as much detail and with as much style as possible, *one* of
the people sitting in the same room as you at the moment. You must
know this person to some extent – it can be yourself, if you want!

In writing this description keep in mind the following aspects: face,
body and figure, dress, facial expressions, physical movements,
habits, moods, abilities, general character.

4.1   Test 2

Describe, in as much detail and with as much style as possible,
yourself, your *boy/girl friend* or *husband/wife*.

In writing this description keep in mind the following aspects: face,
body and figure, gait, dress, facial expressions, physical movements,
habits, moods, abilities, and general character.

4.2   Describing places

As with people, there is a commonly occurring need to describe
places, even if such descriptions are no more than the picking out of a
few salient features of a town, district, or area like a garden or park.
Such descriptions occur informally in personal letters, and more
formally in official letters and reports.

The writing of descriptions of places is fairly difficult to organise
(compared with for example, the description of people) since all
places whether large (town, city or county), or small (park, river
bank, garden, square, beach, forest) are distinctive in layout, and in
the relation of one part to another.

Apart from the lexical items associated with towns and cities
(roads, amenities, public buildings, green areas etc.), or with smaller
areas, the most important language in this unit is that of location and
spatial relations:

locational adverbs:	here, there, everywhere etc., inside, outside
locational prepositions:	over, beyond, in, at, by, near etc.
locational phrases:	to the east, in the centre, in the eastern part of etc.
locational verbs:	is situated, located, found, surrounded by, encloses, surrounds, covers, extends, runs, flows etc.

4.2 Exercises

1 COMPASS POINTS

Use these expressions to complete the descriptive sentences below
about the wildlife park map:

i)   ... to the (west/east etc.) of ...
     ... 25 miles (north/south etc.) of ...
     South-west of ... / ... is north of ...

ii) In the | east part of ...
             | eastern part of ...
             | south ...

iii) Southwards, ...
     Eastwards, ...

A Rowney Hall
B Museum
C Lake
D Railway
E Bird Observatory
F Observation point
G Lion area
H Station
I Monkey colony
J Elephants

a) Rowney Hall is .... the wildlife park.

b) The observation point is .... the bird observatory.

c) The bird observatory is .... of the forest.

d) .... the lake is the station. ....,
   there is an area put aside for lions.

e) The elephants are kept .... side of the park;

   .... this part is an area for monkeys.

f) The road into the wildlife park runs .... towards
   the Hall.

2 POSITION

Use suitable expressions (right, left, opposite, etc.) to complete the description of the town section shown below:

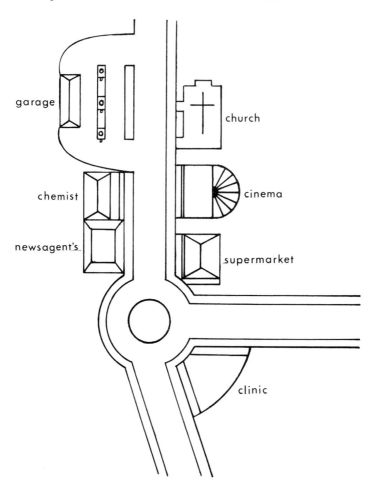

a) The garage is to the .... of the chemist when you're standing outside the church.

b) The chemist is right .... the cinema.

c) The chemist is also .... the garage and the newsagent's.

d) The cinema is right .... the church and quite .... the clinic.

3 Fill in the spaces below with these words (check new words in an English–English dictionary):

industrial estate / one-way-system / landmark / suburbs / area / tourists / centre / tourist attraction / residential areas / riverside / view / residents

> Framley is a small town situated 15 miles east of Bladen. It has one famous ...., the 19th Century Town Hall, a popular ...., which is in the .... of the town. Most people live in the ...., in well-defined ...., and 50% work on the .... by the ....
> Recently the town has adopted a .... which confuses .... and .... alike. A little way out of Framley on Bladen Height there is a fine .... over the whole ....

4 Look at the map of a small town below and then write accurate sentences with these words:

... to the south-east ...   ... right next ...
... not far ...   ... centre ...
... along ...   ... on the corner ...

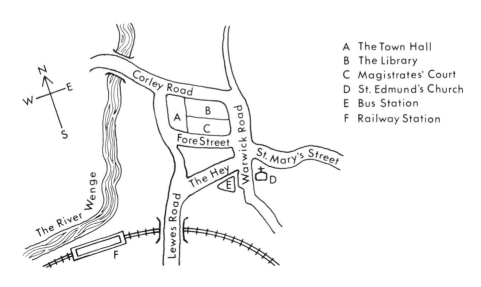

A The Town Hall
B The Library
C Magistrates' Court
D St. Edmund's Church
E Bus Station
F Railway Station

Extra practice

A Descibe *one* of the places suggested below.
Your description should give the reader an idea of the *size*,
location and *type of place* you are writing about.
You should mention interesting or remarkable features.
You should also say how you feel about the town.

Describe the small town or village that you most like being in,
apart from your own!
or
Describe the city or town that you least like being in (but don't
describe your own town!).

B Using the plan below, and its associated key, write a clear
description of the park.
Describe: the layout of the park
the important features of the park

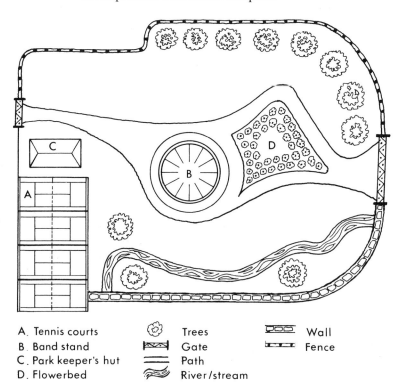

A. Tennis courts   Trees   Wall
B. Band stand   Gate   Fence
C. Park keeper's hut   Path
D. Flowerbed   River/stream

4.2 Test 1

Do both A and B:

A Write a description of the following town, including as much
detail as possible:

B Write a 150-word description of a beach that you know and like.
Give a general idea of the features of the beach and of its size and
extent.

4.2 Test 2

Do both A and B.

A Write a description of Bideford, using the photograph and the
information given below.

BIDEFORD

Pop: 35,000
Location: North Devon, on River
Torridge

Transport: roads to Exeter,
Cornwall, and along coast to Bristol;
railway link to Exeter

Industry and occupations:
boat-building, timber, port,
communications, farming

Buildings: fine bridge, good 17th
and 18th Century merchants' houses

B Write a 150-word description of a park that you know and like.
Give a general idea of the layout of the park and its outstanding
features.

4.3 Describing objects

Foreign users of English may have to write descriptions of objects
which are complete in themselves as for example when placing an
advertisement in a newspaper to sell an object, or producing a written
description of something which has been lost. However, most
descriptions of objects will occur more haphazardly, in personal
letters, and in official letters and reports. The description of objects
may involve an unpredictable amount and type of language in the
following two areas:

i) *quantitative:* number
                     quantity (all, many, half a ...)
                     degree (a lot, hardly, a little)

ii) *qualitative:* shape
    (physical)   size/measurement
                    weight
                    sensory (sight, taste, smell, feel, audibility)
                    colour
                    age
                    condition
                    material

    (evaluative)   value/price
                    quality (good, bad)
                    utility
                    normality (unusual, common)
                    capacity (can/can't)

Descriptions of objects will also involve being able to use the language
of spatial relations effectively (e.g. the control button is quite close to
the aerial on top of the radio).

4.3 Exercises

1 Complete these descriptive sentences:

measurements   The box is 25 cm ...., 6 cm ....

               and has a .... of 6 cm.

weight and   This cheese .... half a kilogram; the ham is 200 grams
   volume
               in ....

               A normal English milk bottle .... about ½ litre of milk.

age   The concert hall is now 21 ....

colour   Some roses are a pale .... colour, some

               deep .... and others yellowy-..................... .

shape   These earrings are ....
               -shaped.
               A tennis ball is .... ; an egg
               is ....

material	The blade of a spade is .... steel; the handle is usually ....
pattern	I have one .... shirt, one .... shirt, and the rest are ...., without a pattern.
sensory	There is nothing in this box – it sounds ....
	The surface of an apple feels .... and it smells ....
	Monthly magazines often have .... covers.
condition	There are holes in my shoes; they are ....
	I need to get some .... ones.
use	A wooden spoon .... stirring soups, serving salads and making bread.
capacity	The aerial on a radio .... extended when needed.

2 Look at the picture of the box below and then say where the numbered points are:

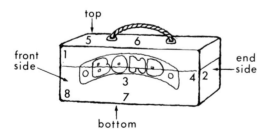

e.g. 1 – in the top left-hand corner on the front.
       2 – in the middle of the right-hand end

Now continue: 3 ..... 4 .....

3 Look at the pictures below and write one sentence about
measurements, use, colour, surface feel, pattern and decoration,
position and place, material.
  It's probably best to start most of your sentences with 'It's . . .'

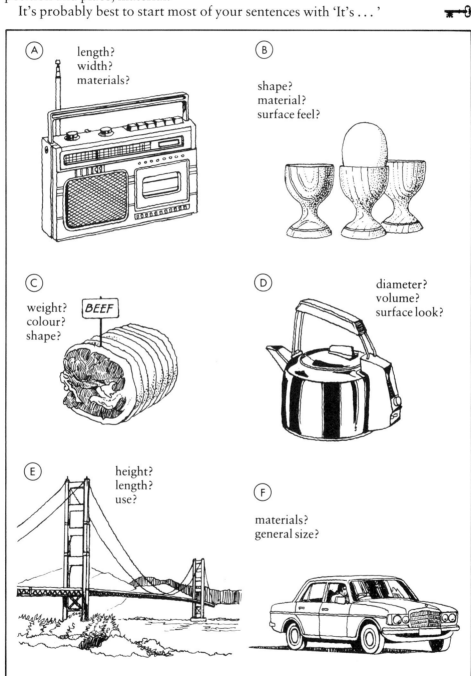

A length?
   width?
   materials?

B shape?
   material?
   surface feel?

C weight?
   colour?
   shape?

   BEEF

D diameter?
   volume?
   surface look?

E height?
   length?
   use?

F materials?
   general size?

Extra practice

Describe the three objects suggested below:

A You have lost your watch. Write a simple description to hand to the caretaker of the building where you lost the watch so that he can try to find it.

B Write a description of this attractive wooden door.

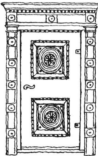

C Write a description of your coffee-pot or water-jug.

4.3 Test 1

Write all three descriptions:

A You've just bought *a dress, shoes, a jacket, a coat*. Write a description to a friend beginning, 'I've just bought this . . .'

B Write a description of the interior of a *theatre, cinema* or *football stadium*. Do *not* describe what is happening – just describe the place.

C Look at the picture below. *Two* of these pieces of furniture have been stolen from you. You must write an advertisement for them in a local paper, describing them in as much detail as possible. Offer a reward for the return of the furniture.

4.3 Test 2

Write all three descriptions:

A You've just bought a *bag, handbag,* or *briefcase.* Write a description to a friend beginning, 'I've bought a ...'

B Write a description of the front of a house you can see or remember.

C Look at the two objects below. Write an advertisement offering a reward for their return after a robbery at your house – describe them as accurately as possible.

4.4 Describing human scenes

This unit is *not* concerned with describing or reporting the past; that sort of written text is dealt with in Section 5 (Units 5.1 and 5.3). Unit 4.4 is devoted to descriptions of present events and scenes. Although this is common in the spoken medium (as commentary) it does not exist as a complete written text-type, apart from when it appears as a verbatim account from the spoken medium. Nevertheless, as is implied in the practice items, people frequently need and want to describe what is happening around them in personal writing.

In order to write about human activity as it happens it is necessary to be able to do the following things:

describe things happening at the moment:	present continuous tense
describe things that have been happening up to the present moment:	present perfect continuous tense
describe things that have happened in the period up to the present:	present perfect simple tense
indicate completeness or its opposite:	already/just/recently/not yet
indicate duration:	for/during/since
describe things that can be 'sensed':	I can feel/see/hear . . .
describe present states:	is/are/have/seems
describe location:	across the road a few yards to the left . . .

The practices are divided into two sections, the first based on pictorial stimuli, the second on imagined contextualised situations.

4.4 Exercises

1 A Look at the picture of the man and the woman with the van and answer the questions with complete sentences.

a) What's the man doing now?
b) What have they been doing?
c) What can you see in the trolley?
d) What is the woman doing?
e) What haven't they done yet?
f) What do you think the man has just said?

B Look at the picture of the woman driving a van of schoolboys
  and answer the questions.

a) Where have the boys been all day?
b) What have the boys been doing?
c) What are the boys doing now?
d) Complete 'One boy has just .... and another
   boy is ....'
e) Complete 'They haven't .... yet.'

2 This is part of a letter from a student to his old teacher. Put the
  right form of the verb in.

```
It ............ (be) really difficult to start this letter
now because such a long time ........... (pass) since I
left.  Ever since my return to Germany I ........... (have)
one thing in mind: to write to you.  But up to now I
............ (not do) anything about it.  So I ...........
(must) make myself do it, and this is the result.  At
present I ........... (work) in a factory all day until I
get my chance to get into Lufthansa.  I ...........
(already find) that factory work ........... (be) boring...
```

3 You are sitting in a room in college or at home doing this. Other
  things are happening in the building you're in. Use the following
  ideas to write about them. Write one sentence for each idea:
  a) ... is still ---ing ...   e) ... can't see ...
  b) ... can hear ...   f) ... has been ... since ...
  c) ... hasn't ... yet.   g) ... have already ...
  d) ... aren't ---ing ...   h) ... in the last minute.

Extra practice

Do both A and B:

A You are staying with this family. As part of a letter to an American friend describe what's going on in this family at the moment.

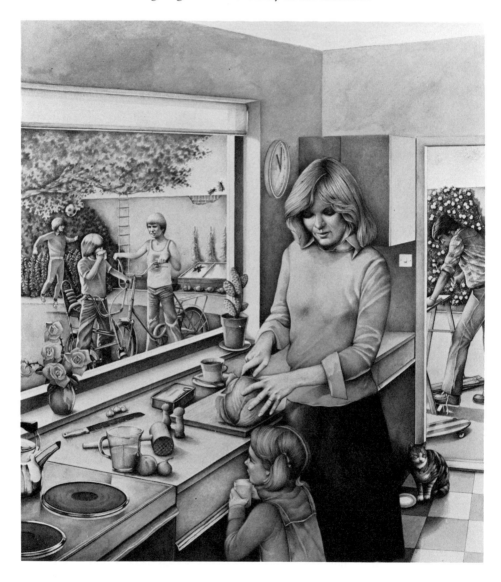

B You are at an airport, waiting for a delayed plane. You decide to kill time by writing to a close friend. Include a description in the letter of what is happening around you at the airport.

4.4 Test 1

Do both A and B:

A Write out the following passage from a letter, putting in the right
tense forms. The girl is now at home, writing this letter:

Dear Nancy,
        I (just return) home to write a letter to you, although at the
moment it (be) very noisy. Ben, the youngest boy (play) with a
train set he (lay) out, and Tom, who (play) quite happily for the
past hour – according to his mother – suddenly (decide) to become
a jet aeroplane and (scream) round the house like Concorde. I
(think) I (hear) the baby girl crying. Mr Roberts (not return) home,
he (probably still work) . . . I (not get) far yet!

B Below you'll find a picture of a garden scene that you can see from
your bedroom window. Describe the scene as fully as possible.

4.4 Test 2

Do both A and B:

A Write out the passage below, putting in the right tense forms. A
man, in the middle of a long plane journey, is writing to a woman:

> ... down below I (see) the tops of some mountains, even though
> the plane (fly) at 16,000 feet ... we (just go) through a cloud, and
> now everyone (look) out of the window, and (stop) talking ... we
> (not fly) half the journey yet, although they (already serve) two
> meals. Ah ... ! The stewardess (appear) and at this very moment
> (bring) me what I (want) ... a cup of black coffee – I (smell) it from
> here! I (hope) they (make) it strong ...

B Below you'll find a picture of a scene on a beach. You are there
too, not far away. Describe the scene as fully as possible.

4.5   Describing landscape

As suggested in the Student's Book (page 71) foreign writers of
English will only need to produce complete and comprehensive
descriptions of landscape if they are involved with the tourist industry
or the production of brochures etc. Nevertheless landscape
descriptions – a term which includes here seascapes and urban
landscapes – may well be part of personal letter-writing. Unlike
descriptions of places which may be organised in a number of
different ways, landscape descriptions are essentially pictorial, and
proceed from the physical point of view of the writer.

   A number of suggestions about language have been made in the
notes in the Student's Book; obviously a number of lexical areas are
important; in addition, the expression of relative position and
distance assume importance in landscape descriptions. A further
important language point relates to the nature of landscape
descriptions: they are essentially descriptions of states, so that verbs
are used in the present universal form:
e.g.   the road bends near the bridge . . .
   the fields go right up to the skyline . . .

N.B.   There is a small stream in the valley, *winding* between . . .

4.5 Exercises

1 DISTANCE AND POSITION

Use these words to complete the passage about the picture:

distance / horizon / middle distance / silhouetted / sunlight / skyline / beyond / across / surrounded by / view

The river winds away into the .... and on the

.... is a line of hills .... against the distant

.... There is a village in the .... ,

.... which there is a small wood. In the centre of the

village there is an old stone church ....

stone cottages. .... the river lies the other half of the

village. Half the scene is still in bright .... and offers a

glowing .... of a Welsh country village.

2 GROUND AND GROUND COVER

Write the numbers from the picture next to the correct description below:

a fence   a line/clump of trees   a line/ridge of hills
a hedge   a marsh   a ridge/range of mountains
a wood   moorland   a ploughed field
a forest   a pond   grazing land
an orchard   a haystack

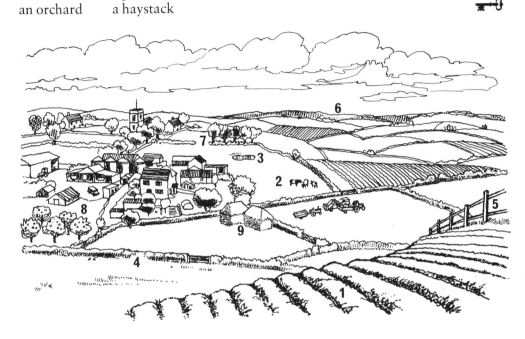

3 WATER

Look at the map below and write on the following words:

river / stream / canal / estuary / lake / pond / weir / banks of a river

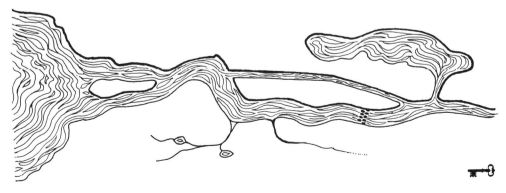

4 SEA AND SEASCAPE

Label the following picture with these words:

headland / bay / cliff / beach / tideline / rockpools / harbour

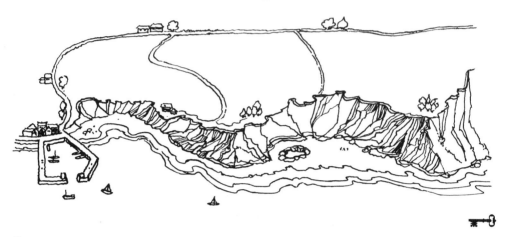

5 ROADS AND PATHS

Use these words to complete the passage below:

footpath / main road / lane, country lane / track / motorway /
alleyway / bridlepath / gate

A fast new .... links Taunton and Exeter but there are

also two other .... connecting the two main towns.

Friends of mine live a little way out of Exeter and to get there one

must drive along a twisting .... for two miles. Another

acquaintance of mine works on a farm which is at the end of a bumpy

dirt .... There are plenty of .... across

Dartmoor but always remember to close the .... after

you. There are also a number of .... for horse riders in

the foothills of Dartmoor. In Exeter itself there are a number of

curious old .... between the old stone buildings.

6 WEATHER AND SKY

Write ten sentences using the table below with the ten weather words.
Then write two true sentences about today.

There is a / It is a / It is	haze / breeze / mist / drizzling / overcast / clear / cloudless / dull / wintry / muggy	today / day today / sky today

7 FEELINGS ABOUT LANDSCAPE

Put a tick (√) or a cross (×) next to these words to show whether they
are negative or positive feelings about a view.

spectacular	picturesque
charming	dismal
melancholy	breath-taking
stirring	depressing
dull	pretty

Which words would you use to describe:
a) a view of the Alps?
b) a view of a small English village?
c) the view from your window?

Extra practice

Do both A and B:

A You're sitting on the bank of the river Dart at Staverton. Describe the scene in front of you.

STAVERTON

B Go to the window of the room you are in: your bedroom, a classroom, or the room with the best view, and then describe the scene from this window.

4.5   Test 1

Write all three descriptions:

A   Write two or three sentences about this scene.
    Ideas: Rhine / bank / castle

B   Write two or three sentences about this scene.

C   Write a *full* description of this landscape, as accurately as you can.

4.5 Test 2

Write all three descriptions:

A Write a few sentences about this river scene.
   Ideas: the river curves / Rhine / steep bank(s)

B Write two or three sentences about this coastal scene.

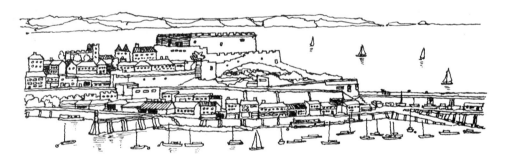

C Write a full and accurate description of the landscape pictured
   below.

4.6 Describing habits and conditions

In all sorts of text-types there may be a need to describe the way
people or civilisations do things, and the way things always happen.
These descriptions may be of the present or the past. Such writing
may occasionally constitute a text-type in its own right, but this is
unlikely outside professional or business writing (current reports,
brochures etc.).

The following are important language categories when writing
about habits or conditions:

describing present habits: present simple tense
                                 phrasal exponents: tend to
                                               a tendency to
                                               have the habit of

expressing frequency: frequency adverbs (e.g. frequently / rarely /
                                     quite often / once a week)

describing past habits: used to do
                              would do
                              always/never did

describing irritating habits: present continuous tense
                                      keeps (on) doing
                                      continues to do

present and past states: simple present and simple past tenses

universal generalisations: present simple tense

Here are some further examples from personal letters of the way
people describe habits and conditions:

'... it's very difficult because we have to go into the hospital every day and
put on our cheerful faces. All this worry means that nothing gets done in the
garden and we probably aren't eating at all properly ...'

'... the most amazing thing about working here is that you start and finish in
the dark. I mean, for most of the year you do anyway. I suppose in the
summer it must almost be the opposite ...'

'... One thing I really miss about the big city is the way you can get or do
anything. I used to be able to nip out of bed for some hot croissants or rolls
or something just round the corner, or go and eat Indian or Russian or
Turkish just when you fancied it. Can't do that here, for all its charm!'

'... What you have to do is order the wood about a month in advance,
(otherwise you won't get it till next year!) and just wait for it to arrive in sort
of metre lengths. Then, when it's there on the pavement, you go and get hold
of a woodcutter, who puffs along in his horribly dangerous-looking machine
and cuts it all up for you for a fee and many glasses of the fiery stuff ...'

4.6 Exercises

1 WORD POSITION

Put the words in brackets in the right place:

a) He watches TV. (every day)
b) They phone me. (never)
c) She eats with her fingers. (never ever)
d) I have a sauna. (once a week)
e) The British eat good fish. (seldom)
f) It rains in London. (frequently)
g) It snows in Devon. (doesn't generally)
h) We have a holiday in August. (almost always)
i) They play a lot of chess. (on Mondays)
j) I see my mother. (somewhat infrequently)

2 'HABIT' WORDS

Look at these descriptive sentences using expressions of habit. Then use the underlined expressions to write seven sentences about yourself, your family, or your friends.

Football crowds <u>tend</u> to be noisy, and have the <u>irritating habit</u> of leaving lots of litter behind them. The shops around my local ground are <u>constantly</u> having their windows smashed in. I suppose some fans have <u>got into the habit</u> of mixing violence with sport and, although football clubs <u>continue</u> to issue warnings in club programmes, stories of football vandalism <u>habitually</u> appear in the press. Consequently, there is a <u>tendency</u> for families to stay away from live football for fear of violence.

4.6 Test 1

Do both A and B:

A Write 60–80 words about your life now compared to your life as a child.

B Describe how people generally travel in your country, mentioning: the transport systems available; their advantages and disadvantages; people's preferences; changing travel habits.

4.6 Test 2

Do both A and B:

A Write a description of how people in your country spend the major religious or public holiday in your culture.

B Very briefly, describe the differences between sporting activity and facilities available now and 50 years ago.

   or

   Describe the differences between a working day now and in your grandparents' time.

4.7 Describing processes

In technical or scientific writing process descriptions are a common feature of texts; the ordinary foreign writer of English is unlikely to need to write technical texts. There are occasions, however, when people need to describe how things happen or how things are done in relatively informal contexts as well. The practice items in this unit are examples of the kinds of contexts where such writing may be required.

Because good process description is relatively difficult to write and requires quite a lot of guidance from teachers and sources, fairly full explanatory language notes have been placed in the Student's Book (page 78). The teacher should refer to these and the exercises that follow.

Writing descriptions

4.7 Exercises

1 People often go into hospital. Lots of things happen to them there:
   a) Unfortunately, they *are* all '*examined*'. (passive voice)
   b) Some *survive*. (active voice)

   Now write sentences from these ideas; start each sentence with *Patients* or *Some patients*:

   c) treat
   d) become worse
   e) give blood transfusions
   f) die
   g) nurse
   h) visit
   i) get well
   j) examine
   k) seem ill

2 What happens to the things in the list below when they are processed or dealt with? Write answers keeping each phrase as the *subject* of your sentences.
   e.g. a) Grapes *Grapes are picked and then used to make wine.*

   b) Cement?
   c) An old battery?
   d) A poor footballer?
   e) An old language laboratory?
   f) Fish?
   g) Coffee beans?
   h) A criminal?

3 Look at these examples:
   ... is done ...   ... does ...
   ... has been done ...   ... has done ...

   Use one of these four forms with the verbs given, in the blanks below:

   '... the sugar .... (add) and the jam soon

   .... (turn) thick. Once it ....

   (become) thick enough to stand a spoon in, it

   .... (pour) into pound jam-jars. As soon as it

   .... (cool) a cellophane disc ....

   (place) on the surface of the jam and the jars ....

   (seal) with more cellophane and rubber bands. The jam

   .... (deteriorate) the longer you keep it so it

   .... (normally eat) within a year of being made ...'

4 Write six sentences using one of the following phrases each time:

by means of   through
using   by
with the help of   involving
through the use of

  e.g. The fruit is cut *by means of* a long-handled knife.
       With the help of his friends he gradually returned to normal
       life.

  a) contact / made / telephone
  b) goods / moved / railways
  c) grapes / picked / local people and students
  d) cars / lifted / jacks
  e) doors / opened / keys
  f) preserving / both salting and freezing / an important part of
      cooking traditions

5 Look at the following ways of introducing the stages in a process:

The first				This	process	begins	with
The	second	step	is to . . .	The		commences	when
	subsequent	stage				finishes	after
	following					concludes	once
The	last						
	final						

During / In the following stage / At the next stage . . .

Write sentences about bread-making, by adding expressions of
staging and sequencing to those below:

1st stage
yeast is mixed with warm water
mixture added to $\frac{1}{2}$ flour, batter is left

2nd stage
rest of flour is added, with salt and oil
dough is kneaded and left

3rd stage
dough is moulded into loaves
loaves are left to rise

4th stage
bread is cooked in very hot oven

Extra practice

Do both A and B:

A Describe the differences between the way tea or coffee is made in your country and in Britain for a curious friend.
   N.B. *Don't* write instructions but a description.

B Describe for a foreign primary school teacher:
   either How children are taught to read and write in schools in your country.

   or   What methods are used to teach children/adults their first foreign language in your country.

4.7   Test 1

Do A or B:

You have a friend of a different nationality and language who is very interested in politics. He/she is shortly coming to your country and wants to know two things:

A The process by which people become political representatives.

B The process by which a president or prime minister achieves power in your country.

4.7   Test 2

Do A or B:

A An American friend of yours wants to attend a university in your country. Describe the process by which he/she may enrol at a university as a foreign student.

B A British friend wishes to open a bank account in your country. Describe the procedures he/she has to go through in order to do this.

Section 5 Reporting experiences

Introduction

The units in this section all share one feature: they describe and report life as it was once. Such reports may be self-contained as for example in the short story, the written anecdote, or the accident report; for the normal user of a foreign language, however, reporting experiences is frequently part of something else, particularly in personal letter-writing. A second point to note about this section is that although it is entitled *reporting* experiences, it is almost impossible to find reports of past events and activities that do not include elements of past *description*, a mixture, in other words of dynamic and stative writing about the past.

All reporting shares the rhetorical feature of sequencing: reporting is essentially the provision of a sequentially-ordered account of events even though comment, evaluation and description may be added to this sequence.

The language that students will need to use for reporting experiences will be in these areas:

i) expressing the past (reporting completed actions, describing incomplete or interrupted actions, describing habits, conditions and states, offering past hypotheses)

ii) sequencing the past (using past and pre-past tenses in relation; using conjunctions and conjuncts as sequencing devices; using participles)

5.1 Reporting incidents and events

Apart from accident or incident reports made for official purposes, this sort of writing is rarely a self-contained text-type but occurs within other kinds of writing text, particularly informal letter-writing. On the whole the reporting of incidents or events involves sequencing actions in the past, with the addition of necessary descriptive detail.

The language needed to do this is summarised below:

reporting action: simple past

describing the past: simple past (was, discovered)
interrupted/unfinished action (was doing)

sequencing: conjunctions (before/after/as soon as)
pre-past action (had done)
interrupted/incomplete pre-past (had been doing)
conjuncts (After that, ... following this, ...)

past hypotheses: e.g. 'He would have ... if she had done ... '

causal connections: purpose
reason (conjunctions and conjuncts)
result

5.1   Exercises

1 For each sentence choose the right form from those in the brackets.
When you make your choice remember that this will depend
on (a) whether the action was complete or incomplete, and
(b) whether the action was in simple past time, or a time *before* a
simple past time.

a) I knew you (talked/were talking/had been talking) about me by
the guilty look on your faces when I (arrived/was arriving/had
been arriving).
b) What really (had happened / happened / was happening)
yesterday morning?
c) I (popped in / was popping in / had popped in) from time to
time to talk to her throughout the weekend.
d) She (never ate / had never eaten / was never eating) spaghetti
before that.
e) When she (was seeing him / saw him / had been seeing him) she
quickly left.
f) We (laughed / had laughed / were laughing) when to our horror
he suddenly dropped down dead.
g) There was a smell of cigarette smoke in the empty room
because someone (was smoking / smoked / had been smoking)
there.
h) He (had watched / watched / was watching) the Olympics on
TV when his sister telephoned. He switched the set off at once.

2 Using the verb in brackets, write the best verb form for each blank
  space.

As soon as I got home, my brother .... (rush) out of

the kitchen. This .... (be) surprising because he

.... (only do) this once before. Up to this day my

brother .... (be always slumped) in his chair at

six, watching the news. So what .... (be) special about

this particular night? Well, sometime earlier in the day he

.... (find) a job! Apparently, five minutes before he

.... (be) due to turn up at the local Job Centre, an old

friend .... (ring) him up to ask if he .... (want)

a job sailing ferries for the summer. He .... (say) 'yes', of

course. So he .... (be) busy for the rest of afternoon

getting his things in order. If he .... (go) out earlier to the

Job Centre he .... (miss) the call and probably

.... (not get) the job.

3 Making time connections is quite important when you are
  reporting incidents and events. In the exercise that follows some
  time words (conjunctions) have been underlined. Complete the
  sentences in a sensible way. (Use a complete verb in the part you
  write.)

a) People stare at that lady <u>whenever</u> ...
b) <u>When</u> Mandy told me about her father's death, ...
c) David phoned the hospital <u>as soon as</u> ...
d) <u>After</u> he had visited the old lady, ...
e) I learned to speak <u>before</u> ...
f) My landlady goes to bed <u>directly</u> ...
g) <u>Immediately</u> the doorbell rang, ...
h) <u>As long as</u> you don't overwork, ...
i) I haven't seen Herman <u>since</u> ...
j) He was able to speak fairly good Spanish <u>once</u> ...
k) <u>The moment that</u> he left school, my father ...
l) She refused to speak to me <u>until</u> ...
m) <u>Every time</u> I go to France ...
n) He phoned her every day <u>while</u> ...
o) You should speak good English <u>now that</u> ...

Extra practice

Do both A and B:

A Report the event you see pictured here. Below you will find some words and ideas to help you.

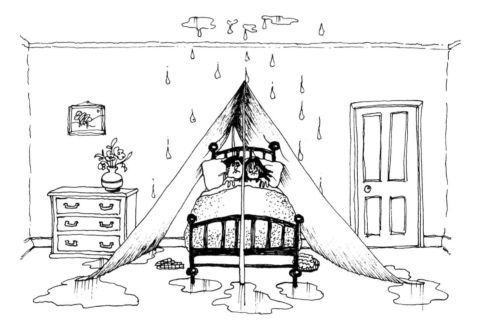

   Ideas: old country cottage – romantic weekend – weather! – no
   phone – leaky roof – damp – flu
   Start: 'A couple of years ago some friends of mine, who hadn't
   been married for very long, decided . . .'

B Describe an incident at a football match when the 'away' side
   scored a goal, the goalscorer was 'punched', and the home crowd
   invaded the pitch (looking dangerous!).
   or
   Report an event in the theatre last year, when the actors began to
   insult their audience (as part of the play) and a number of the
   audience got rather upset and agitated.

5.1   Test 1

Write all three accounts:

A   Report the following incident from the cues:
three a.m. / Robert Filey / hungry / nothing to eat all day /
downstairs / fell / woke father / knife / dark / stabbed – almost
died / father – heart-attack . . .

B   Describe any incident that you have been involved in, or a friend or
relation of yours has been involved in, with one of the following:

police
customs
tax-officials
teachers

C   Report the incident you can see in the picture below as
interestingly as possible:

5.1   Test 2

Write all three reports:

A Report the following incident from the cues below:
   Jill return home / boy friend not there / phone / boy friend on
   way home / long wait – worried / phone police / boy friend
   suddenly . . . / long argument . . .

B Report the incident you can see in the picture below, as
   interestingly as possible:

C There is a diagram of an accident below; a car hit a bus and three
   people died. Write a short account of the accident, starting, 'Two
   cars were waiting at the traffic lights in Lownes Road when . . . '

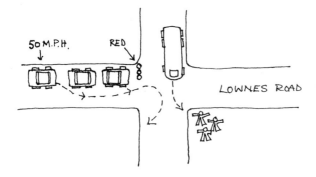

5.2   Writing biographical information

As in Unit 5.1, this sort of writing may well occur in formal reports, particularly official requests for personal testimonials. More commonly a foreign student will need to do this sort of writing within the confines of an informal letter.

Much the same can be said about the language required to write about people in the past as has been said about reporting incidents and events. However, there is a category of lexical items that biographical writing entails, and which are used to describe the events in human life:

he was born / educated / brought up / sent to

she first . . .
     last . . .

he became / grew / turned . . .

She became engaged / got married / had a child / got divorced / retired / died . . .

The sequencing of biographical information is commonly achieved by stating actual dates:

In 1978, . . .
On the 4th March, 1965 . . .
During the next ten years . . .

Sequencing by reference to events *before*, *after*, or *at the same time as* other events is the same as in other kinds of past reporting.

Extra practice

Do both A and B:

A Write an imaginary life-story from the following notes on Andrew Faulds:

LONDON
* born 1951
* father died (when 3)
* two sisters – older
* good at English, art at school
* loved football
* school newspaper

COVENTRY
* 1971 Art College – art and design
* editor, college magazine
* cartoons

LEEDS
* 1974 job on Leeds evening paper
* married
* 1976 freelance cartoonist

B Interview a person you live with, take notes and write up their life-story so far.
or
Write up the life-story of one of your parents: your mother or your father.

5.2   Test 1

Do both A and B.

A In about 50 words, write an outline of your own life so far.

B Think of a famous entertainer who is still alive today. He or she
may be of any nationality. Suppose that this person died today:
write the obituary that would appear in tomorrow's newspaper.

5.2   Test 2

Do both A and B.

A In about 60 words, write a very brief outline of the life of your
President or Prime Minister.

B Write a clear biographical account of your grandfather *or*
grandmother, *or* a close family friend. Mention ordinary family
details; also mention interesting events.

5.3   Narrating

Few students of English are likely to want to write complete
narratives in a foreign language. This unit is for the few who do, or
for those who for some other reason, such as the types of examination
question they may face, need to be able to write complete narratives.
The unit is divided into historical or true narrative and fictional
narrative. Obviously, the writing of narrative, whether fictional or
historical, will involve both report and description, i.e. action and
descriptive background to action.

As far as language requirements are concerned everything said in
the introduction to this section, and the comments made on Units 5.1
and 5.2, is relevant to this unit. There is a list of useful language
points in the language notes section of the Student's Book.

N.B.   For those students who have chosen to write a continuation of
the story which begins in the model on page 90 of the Student's Book,
the original version will be found in the Key on page 163.

Extra practice 1

This practice should follow Practices 1 and 2 in the Student's Book, fictional narrative. Do both A and B.

A Write out a fairly simple account of a supernatural or ghost story that you're familiar with, of not more than 150 words, in clear, simple English.

B The sequence of pictures tells a story and there is some information which should help you to organise the narrative.
   You may like to start with this idea:

'Like a lot of children her age – which was just 14 – Lucy always went straight off to the local sweet shop when she came out of school. Monday, 3rd March was no different. After school she . . .'

Extra practice 2

This practice of factual narrative reporting should follow Practices 3 and 4 in the Student's Book. Do both parts. Part A is about something you are familiar with and Part B asks you to practise narrative using supplied material.

WAR

A All countries have, at some time in their history, been involved in a war with another country. Look back through the history of your country and describe *one war* in which your country was involved.

MAN ON THE MOON

B Using the material supplied below, write an account of how man eventually got to the moon.

1961 President Kennedy said: 'I believe that this nation should commit itself to achieving the goal, before this decade is out, of landing a man successfully on the Moon and returning him safely to Earth.'

1961-9 Apollo space programme developed.
Apollo spacecraft mounted on Saturn V, rockets launched.

1962 Apollo 1 crashed – astronauts Grisson, White and Chaffee killed. Russian astronaut, Komarov killed – spaceship came back to earth too fast – burnt up.

1962-8 Apollo spacecraft 2-7 tested out in space.

December 1968 Apollo 8 – ten orbits round Moon – safely back to Earth.

May 1969 Apollo 10 – final rehearsal for Moon landing – successful Moon landing – return to earth.

1968-9 Three astronauts in intensive training for Moon trip: Neil Armstrong, Buzz Aldrin, Michael Collins.

July 16, 1969 Apollo 11 launched with three astronauts – no problems – 15,000 miles per hour – directed by computers.
70 miles above Moon's surface, two parts of spacecraft (lunar module 'Eagle' and command module 'Columbia') went into orbit of Moon. 'Eagle' launched from command module – Armstrong and Aldrin land on Moon.
Armstrong 'That's one small step for man, one giant leap for mankind.'
Armstrong and Aldrin returned to command module.
Safe return to Earth.

5.3   Test 1

Do both A (fictional narrative) and B (factual narrative).

A   In the bubbles below, there is a dream sequence in pictures which Alison once had. Narrate the dream beginning in the following way:

'Alison once had a dream which began when she found herself at a party ...'

B Write out a narrative of how Robert Scott reached the South Pole.

27th Nov. 1910	Robert Scott left Dunedin, New Zealand in ship *Terra Nova* plus food, equipment, Husky dogs, ponies, sledges, 60 men.
early Jan. 1911	Terrible storms; landed on Antarctica (Hurrah Beach); killer whales killed some ponies; crew built base.
from Feb. onwards	Depots from Hurrah Beach to South Pole.
early 1912	Scott's small party reached South Pole (found Norwegian Amundsen had got there first, 15 December, 1911 – very depressed by this). Started journey back; weather awful; clinging snow slowed down; food running out; one man died; another disappeared; rest died; 11 miles from depot.

5.3 Test 2

Do both A (fictional narrative) and B (factual narrative).

A Think of a *novel* or a *play* with a good, clear story. In less than 250 words, write a clear, narrative outline of the novel or play you have chosen.

B Using the information given below, write a clear account of how and why Henry VIII of England married six different women.

1509	Henry VIII, King of England, age 17 England, Roman Catholic country
1510	Henry VII (father) had arranged marriage with Catherine of Aragon (Henry VIII's brother's widow!) Political marriage
1516	Daughter (Mary Tudor)
1520	Henry VIII – many mistresses at Court – one illegitimate son
1533	Divorced Catherine of Aragon – no son
1533	Married Anne Boleyn – unpleasant woman – in secret, in January September daughter born – Elizabeth I
1536	Catherine of Aragon died Ann Boleyn executed for treason (hadn't produced a son?) Married Jane Seymour
1537	Jane Seymour died – son born (Edward VI)
1540	Married Anne of Cleves (had seen beautiful picture of her) Divorced Anne of Cleves – actually very ugly
1540	Married Catherine Howard
1542	Catherine Howard executed for treason
1543	Married Catherine Parr
1547	Henry VIII died
1548	Catherine Parr died

5.4 Reporting speech

In informal writing this activity is even less of a single text-type than
the other units in this section. Reported speech does occur as a
text-type however, in the form of minutes of a meeting, or a summary
report (cf Unit 7.3, Practice 3).

The success of speech reporting depends upon linguistic ability in
the following areas:

using appropriate 'speech' verbs and the right structures with them:
   (deny, state, comment, mention)

reporting speech: verb tenses   ('I am ... '; he said he was ...)
                     references to people   (John: 'You are right'; John
                        told him he was right.)
                     references to time   ('tomorrow'; the day after)
                     references to place   ('there'; the adjacent seat)

Practice in these areas is offered in the language exercises.

5.4 Exercises

Do *all* the exercises here.
1 Look at these examples and then report the statements below from
   a programme on the radio called 'Modern Marriage'.

   e.g. 1 'Mugging is a modern urban crime.'
               He stated that mugging was a modern urban crime.
         2 'It has not got out of control.'
               He denied that it had got out of control.
         3 'The public can help to fight it.'
               He suggested that the public could help to fight it.

   a) ... marriage is still important ...   (She stated ...)
   b) ... but has many enemies ...   (She claimed ...)
   c) ... as women's roles change ...   (She suggested ...)
        ... marriage is becoming less easy ...
   d) ... marital roles have begun to change ...   (She said ...)
   e) ... they'll change further of course ...   (She added ...)
   f) ... but women will still be having babies in 50 years' time ...
        (She stated ...)
   g) ... so marriage can't possibly disappear!   (She denied ...)
   h) ... it began from necessity ...   (She explained ...)
   i) ... it's going to remain from necessity ...   (She continued ...)

2 Report these statements, questions and denials:

    e.g. 1 'I saw you.'
                She told him she had seen him.
         2 'Did you see me?'
                She asked him if he had seen her.

The speaker can be a man or a woman.

a) I don't like him.
b) Do you?
c) Do you want a drink?
d) I have never drunk alcohol.
e) He won't drink with me.
f) Is it immoral?
g) Could you explain that?
h) Where were you born?
i) I mightn't come.
j) Have you finished?
k) What did he do?
l) I won't have to work if I stay in England.

3 In this exercise choose the right verb each time. Make sure you carefully check the meaning of the words you don't understand.

The boss | asked / doubted / thought | if we had any ideas. I | denied / proclaimed / suggested | that

we should reduce the number of staff. He | revealed / added / advised | that this had

been done already, but | instructed / doubted / added | he didn't really like this.

Robin then | said / spoke and seemed to / told | mention / imply / realise | that the only hope

was to expand. He | advised / informed / claimed | we hadn't expanded for five years.

Extra practice

Write all three reports:

A The following is a discussion in a pub. Report it as concisely as you can:

Robin: Of course, women will always look to men as the dominant sex ...

Anna: What's that?

Robin: They always have done so, and will go on doing so – it's the natural order of things ...

Anna: Ha! Let me tell you that ...

Robin: Hang on, I haven't finished yet ...

Anna: Just shut up. I'm going to fill your ears with news you won't like ... First the idea of women being submissive has always been and was from the beginning a male idea; secondly, now we know that one woman can be a Prime Minister, or a pianist, or a chess player, we know that all can, and ...

Robin: Nothing of the sort! Women have been writing poems for hundreds of years, some *can* write very well but on the whole great poets are usually men. The fact that the occasional woman becomes great is no reason to suppose that they are not – generally – the submissive sex. Anything to add?

Anna: Yes. You're a prejudiced pig, and I'm not going to speak to you for the next ... 10 minutes.

B In the conversation above:
Who asserted what?
Who denied what?
Who went on to say what?

C Think of things your mother/father/friends have

suggested	denied
warned	doubted
implied	wondered

in the last few weeks.

Write down sentences including each of the verbs.

5.4   Test 1

Do both A and B:

A Read this conversation between a father and his daughter:

F: People in Europe are far, far happier than they were at the turn of the century.

D: Can you be so sure of that?

F: Sure – I ... know it ... I've seen it. (*Pause*) Go into the street and compare what you can see now with press photos from 1900 ...

D: Photos aren't necessarily good evidence of happiness, are they!

F: Anne! (his wife) Anne! – bring the book of press-cuttings will you? I'll show this 20-year-old a thing or two!

Now report the conversation using these words:

asserted	insisted
questioned	suggested
added	asked
promised	doubted

B Write a report of the conversation which remains in your memory most strongly of those below:

i)   A recent conversation with your parents/friends.

ii) A recent meal-time conversation.

iii) A recent conversation in a pub or a restaurant.

5.4 Test 2

Do both A and B:

A Read this short conversation between two strangers in a pub:

    1: Excuse me, I wonder if you could moderate your language a bit.
    2: I beg your pardon?
    1: Well, not everyone wants to hear your ... jokes.
    2: Move away, then!
    1: I don't see why I should ... your language is rather vulgar, that's all.
    2: There's another bar the other side of that door. You're a bit delicate!

Now report the conversation in writing for evidence in a court of law. These speech words might be useful:

requested	asserted
asked	added
stated	mentioned
suggested	

B Write a report on one of the following:
    i)   An interview or part of an interview for a job you once had.
    ii) A conversation you remember with a teacher or a headmaster.
    iii) A conversation with one of your grandparents about something in their life.

Section 6 Writing to companies and officials

Introduction

This section covers writing that has been called by Widdowson and Davies (*Edinburgh Course in Applied Linguistics* Vol. 3) 'institutional writing' as opposed to personal writing. In many ways, these are the easiest texts for students to learn to write since they arise from very precise needs, and achieve their ends by an economy of means in the form of particular phrases and formulas. Students often see such writing as more genuinely essential than other sorts of writing. Filling in forms, writing request letters, giving and asking for information has direct relevance to how a person functions in a foreign society.

It must be stressed that this section is only concerned with how an individual writes to officials and companies; the question of how to write business correspondence, i.e. company to company or company to individual, is not touched on in this book.

The conventions that govern the layout and presentation of letters to officials and companies in Units 6.2 to 6.7 are set out in the introduction section of the Student's Book, with relevant language notes: these cover address forms, salutation, the writing of dates, and general layout features. Although there may be small differences in the way English-speaking people do these things, the models and suggestions made in this book will be quite adequate for students wishing to write these sorts of letters. Students should certainly be reassured that 'flowery' language is not necessary in English official letter-writing; indeed, such language may actually irritate or be regarded as insincere by those in receipt of letters which contain it; there is a great difference between simple politeness and gratuitous flattery or self-abasement.

There is probably more predictable language available to the writer of official letters than in some other units, and less need to describe and report in original ways. Hence, students often require little more than an adequate functional repertoire to meet the purposes of each kind of letter suggested. This repertoire is suggested in the language notes to each unit in the Student's Book.

N.B. It may be valuable for teachers to build up collections of similar texts to use as supplementary materials.

These text-types are fairly easy for students to cope with and the following notes are correspondingly brief.

6.1 Form-filling

Although all forms are unique, the language that they use to obtain
information is not. Thus the model in the Student's Book has been
used to offer a fairly full list of the language found on the majority of
forms. Three sorts of forms are a common part of everyday life: forms
requesting general information, forms involving money, and
application forms.

  The only advice one would wish to offer foreign writers of English
would be that they write clearly (and in capitals if requested) and that
when requested by forms to give 'brief details' that they avail
themselves of the elliptical devices available to English writers
(cf Section 3 Units 1 and 2).

N.B. Teachers should make enough copies of the forms for their
students, or get the students to copy the forms themselves.

Extra practice 1: Sending for things (by post)

Fill in *all* five forms:

A

Send to Holimarine, Dept. S (TR03) PO Box 2, Bilston, West Midlands WV14 9LD.
Or phone our 24 hour Brochafone Service on Sedgley [STD 090 73] 77235/6.

INITIALS   SURNAME

NAME: MR/MRS/MISS

ADDRESS:

Holimarine

B

So please show me how to get quick, reliable, clean copies, without any wasteful interleaving – send me my free Idem Carbonless Paper Demonstration Pack which simply demonstrates all the advantages of Idem, in a choice of blue or black copy – and tells me how my printer can make them work for me.

IDEM, is a trade mark of Wiggins Teape (UK) PLC

To: Wiggins Teape (Mill Sales) Limited, IDEM Division.
Freepost, Basingstoke, Hampshire RG21 2EE. Tel: (0256) 20262

Please send me – free and without obligation – my sample demonstration pack.

Name

Position

Company Name

Address

OB/E/3

SPECIMEN

C

To: Dept. RT, Selective Marketplace Ltd, Belton Road West Extn., Loughborough, Leics., LE11 0XL. Please send me _____silk shirts at £14.95 each including P&P and _____suits at £27.95 each including P&P. I enclose my cheque (with name and address on the reverse side) for £_____ made payable to Selective Marketplace Ltd, or debit my Access/Barclaycard number _____

Please indicate size and colour by ticking appropriate column.

Silk Shirt Size/ Bust Size	(1)34	(2) 36	(3)38	(4)40	2nd Colour Choice
(A) Cream					
(B) Grey					
(C) Peach					
Suit Size/ Bust Size	(5)34	(6)36	(7)38	(8)40	2nd Colour Choice
(D) Grey					
(E) Beige					

Signature _____

Print Name _____

Address _____

_____

_____

Postcode _____

OFFERS OPEN TO UK RESIDENTS ONLY. PLEASE ALLOW 30 DAYS FOR DELIVERY. REG. OFFICE: BELTON ROAD WEST EXTN., LOUGHBOROUGH, LEICS., LE11 0XL

D

TO: R. J. WILTSHIRE (**OB**)
56-58 Green Street, London, E7.
Please send me

Leather Briefcase(s)_____ Rich Black with Grey Interior

Leather Briefcase(s)_____ Old Burgundy with matching Interior
at £36 (inc. £1.05 carr. & ins. per case).
Please emboss the following initials (max. 4) ___ ___ ___ ___

I enclose cheque/postal order for £ _____ or debit
my Access/Diners Club/Barclaycard/American Express.

My Card No. is: | | | | | | | | | | | | | | | |

BLOCK LETTERS PLEASE

SIGNATURE _____

NAME _____

ADDRESS _____
_____

*CREDIT CARD HOLDERS can order by telephone by ringing
01-472 2192 Mon to Sat 9am to 5pm (orders taken by answerphone
at all other times).*

E

Send to: Wales Tourist Board, Dept. M3, P.O. Box 151,
WDO, Cardiff, CF5 1XS.

✂

Please send me:
☐ Wales – Where to Stay, Hotels and Guest Houses 85p
☐ Wales – Where to Stay, Self-Catering 85p
☐ Walking £1.35
☐ Wales Tourist Map 65p
☐ Castles and Historic Places £1.10
☐ Wales – A Glimpse of the Past £1.00

Remittance   Cheque, postal or
enclosed £_____ money order no _____

Name _____

Address _____

_____ Post Code _____

Extra practice 2: *Money: banks, insurance and assurance*

Fill in *all* the forms below:

A A cheque, drawn on a British bank.

B

HOW TO APPLY

1 Fill in the requested information.

2 Mark a cross against the number of units you require.

3 Sign and date your application.

4 If **YOUR SPOUSE** would also like a Seniorplan Policy to review, please provide information requested under Item 4.

5 Post the Application with your £1 registration fee to the address below. *If you are requesting a Policy for your spouse, please enclose an additional £1.* Send cash, or cheque/ P.O made payable to 'Seniorplan Administrator'.

No stamp required.

SAI
FREEPOST
LIGHTWATER, SURREY. GU18 5BR
Attn: Seniorplan Administrator

APPLICATION FORM
for your Seniorplan.

You are *Guaranteed* to be accepted for this life insurance if you are aged between 50 and 72 and reply during this enrolment period.

YES! Please send me Seniorplan for the number of units requested. I am between 50 and 72. My £1 registration fee is enclosed for my first month's cover. I understand that I will have the opportunity to review my Seniorplan policy in the privacy of my own home. I can return it within 10 days for any reason and you will promptly refund my £1. I also understand that no medical examination is necessary and that I will not be asked a single health question.

BLOCK CAPITALS PLEASE

1 MR MRS MISS Surname _____

First names _____

Address _____

Town _____

County _____ Post Code _____

Date of Birth___/___/___/___ SEX ☐ Male ☐ Female
Day Month Year Age

2 Select the number of units of cover you require by marking with a cross in the appropriate box.

☐ **5 UNITS** £12.75 per month ☐ **4 UNITS** £10.30 per month ☐ **3 UNITS** £7.85 per month ☐ **2 UNITS** £5.40 per month ☐ **1 UNIT** £2.95 per month

3 Signature _____ Date _____

4 _____

If your wife (or husband) would like to apply for Seniorplan please ask her or him to complete the following details:–

MR MRS Surname _____

First names _____

Date of Birth___/___/___/___ SEX ☐ Male ☐ Female
Day Month Year Age

Number of units required (maximum of 5) _____

Signature _____ Date _____

5 Address your envelope and post today to:–
SAI; FREEPOST, Mark House, The Square, Lightwater, Surrey GU18 5BR
(Attn: Seniorplan Administrator)

Lloyd's life *Seniorplan*

RT1

C

TO: TIME ASSURANCE SOCIETY, **FREEPOST**, LONDON EC4B 4TA.
Tel: 01-236 7075/6/7. Please send me, without obligation, your Guide to Personal Pensions, together with a personal illustration.   (BLOCK CAPITALS PLEASE)

Name (Mr/Mrs/Miss) _____

Full Postal Address _____

_____

Occupation _____ Date of birth _____

Age _____

Time Assurance

RT/1/2/79

The Personal Pension Specialists

D

Ansvar

To: Ansvar Insurance Co. Ltd Ansvar House
St Leonards Road, Eastbourne, Sussex   Tel. (0323) 37541
Please send me a quotation for my car insurance.
I am a non-drinker.

Name _____
BLOCK CAPITALS
Address _____

_____

Occupation   Birth date

Make of car [   ]   Model [   ]

Engine capacity [   ]   Year of make [   ]

My present policy expires on [   ]

I will be entitled to [   ] years No Claim Bonus

Will the car be used for business purposes?   Yes [ ] No

Do you wish to bear first £25 of own damage? Yes [ ] No
or first £50 of own damage? Yes [ ] No

Do you require:

*Comprehensive/Third party fire & theft/Third party
*Any driver/Husband & wife only/Insured only

*Delete where applicable   R5

E

Available only to persons permanently residing in England, Scotland, Wales, the Channel Islands or the Isle of Man.

REQUEST FOR QUOTATION Please answer all questions

50⁺ Motorist Plan

Facts about yourself PLEASE USE BLOCK CAPITALS

Mr Mrs Miss	Forenames	Surname

Street Address

Town

County	Postcode

Facts about your car

Make of car	
Model (state if GT, GL, etc)	
Engine capacity	
Year of manufacture	
Registered letters and number	
Estimated mileage for next 12 months	

Who will drive the car? Give details of each person including your own.

Forename(s)	Surname	Age	No. of years full UK Driving Licence held
YOURSELF ⟶			

Have you or any of the named drivers: (Tick appropriate answer) YES* NO

A) been involved in any accident or loss during the past three years? A ☐

B) had any conviction during the past three years for an offence in connection with a motor vehicle (other than parking or one speeding offence) or a driving licence suspension at any time or are there any prosecutions pending? B ☐

C) been refused motor vehicle insurance or continuance thereof at any time? C ☐

D) suffered from diabetes, epilepsy, heart condition, or any other physical or mental disability, infirmity or disease or any condition necessitating use of drugs or mechanical aids? D ☐

*IMPORTANT. If 'yes' to any above questions please give full details and dates separately.

Is the car used: (Commercial travelling, hiring, motor trade excluded) YES NO

A) for journeys to and from work by you or any other person on more than 2 days per week? A ☐

B) by you in person for business purposes? B ☐

C) by any other named driver for business purposes? C ☐

Present Insurance

	Day	Month	Year	
My present policy expires on				**531MT**

At last renewal I was entitled to   years No Claim Discount

Name of present insurer

Please give current/renewal premium (if known) £

Second car? Tick box if you would like an additional Quotation Form ☐
If you would prefer us to send the quotation to your Broker please give his name and address.

SUN ALLIANCE INSURANCE GROUP

No postage stamp needed!
Return today to: Sun Alliance Insurance Group, Dept. MMU, FREEPOST, Horsham RH12 1ZA.

109

Extra practice 3: Education application form

(This practice should follow 6.1, Practice 3)

You have been sent information and also an application form for an intensive weekend course entitled 'Imagination and Reality'. There are lectures, workshops, and seminar sessions. You wish to attend. Fill in the form below.

IMAGINATION AND REALITY   Application Form

Personal Section (please write in block capitals)

MR/MRS/MISS/MS ....

ADDRESS ....

Age [   ] ....

.... Post Code ....

Interests
a) What professional interest do you have in the worlds of Music, Art, Literature, or Drama?

b) What experience as a student do you have of these fields?

c) What are your reasons for wanting to attend Imagination and Reality?

Weekend Options
Participants will be able to choose items from list A or B as long as they are not numbered similarly. Please tick events you want to attend.

MUSIC/ART (A)		**DRAMA/LITERATURE** (B)	
1. Lecture: Contemporary aesthetics	O	1. Presentation: Place of fantasy	O
2. Creative Workshop – Music	O	2. Workshop: Drama and reality	O
3. Seminar – Painter at work	O	3. Workshop – Poetry of crisis	O
4. Workshop– Painting what you see	O	4. Seminar – The writer in and out of his tower	O
5. Seminar – Imagination's uses for the composer	O	5. Seminar – Across the boards	O
6. Workshop: Escape from the literal	O	6. Workshop – Language and reality	O

Costs (Please fill in as appropriate)   Totals £

WORKSHOPS (£6 each)   A2 ☐   A4 ☐   A6 ☐   B2 ☐   B3 ☐   B6 ☐   [   ]
LECTURES (£3)   A1 ☐   B1 ☐   [   ]
SEMINARS (£5 each)   A3 ☐   A5 ☐   B4 ☐   B5 ☐   [   ]
BED & BREAKFAST (£12)   Fri/Sat ☐   Sat/Sun ☐   Sun/Mon ☐   [   ]
LUNCH (£3)   Sat ☐   Sun ☐   [   ]
DINNER (£6)   Fri ☐   Sat ☐   Sun ☐   [   ]

I enclose a deposit of £15 and will forward the balance by 15th March.   [   ]

Signature ....   Date ....

Extra practice 4: *Job application forms*

(This practice should follow 6.1, Practice 4)

A travel company in your country has just advertised for a courier to look after English-speaking tourists on visits to your country. You answered the advertisement and this is the form you have to fill in.

Personal details
NAME . . . .
ADDRESS . . . .
DATE of BIRTH . . . . AGE . . . .
HEALTH (please declare whether you have any disease or disability)
. . . .

Education and work experience
SCHOOLING – List schools from the age of 12 on with dates
1. . . . .
2. . . . .
3. . . . .
4. . . . .
UNIVERSITY/COLLEGE/INSTITUTE – List in order with dates
1. . . . .
2. . . . .
3. . . . .
4. . . . .
EDUCATIONAL CERTIFICATES, DIPLOMAS, DEGREES – List with dates
1. . . . .
2. . . . .
3. . . . .
4. . . . .
OCCUPATION AFTER EDUCATION – List in order with name of employer and dates
1. . . . .
. . . .
2. . . . .
. . . .
3. . . . .
. . . .
4. . . . .
. . . .
5. . . . .
. . . .

English Language
State your proficiency at English. . . . .
What examinations have you passed in English?
. . . .

Courier
Have you been a courier with a travel company before? . . . .
If so, please provide details . . . .
. . . .
Why do you think you would make a good courier?. . . . .
. . . .
. . . .

6.2 Request letters

Request letters to officials and companies are very common – and for the foreign student perhaps the most frequent text-type he or she has to write. Requests may be made for goods or services on the one hand, and information of various sorts on the other. Request letters will usually contain two features: an explanation of circumstances surrounding the request and the request itself.

Adequate language notes have been appended in the Student's Book (page 116). In formal letters of this sort the question of informal request forms does not arise. However, more tentative request forms may be used when the request is seen as more difficult to accede to or of a more delicate nature.

One other formal ability a student needs is that of using indirect question forms in English.

e.g. I would be grateful if you could tell me | where the building is ...
how long it takes ...
whether you intend to ...

Extra practice 1: Requests for goods and services

(This practice should follow 6.2, Practices 1 and 2)

Write *one* letter:

A   You have just moved into a flat in a British or American town. There's no telephone and you use the telephone a lot. Write to the Post Office requesting the installation of a new telephone. Request details of the approximate cost of the phone and its installation.

B   Your new flat has very little furniture. You've just seen an advertisement in a British magazine for some large floor cushions:

FABULOUS CUSHIONS OFFER!

SIZES
32cm×60cm
50cm round
65cm×90cm

COLOURS
Rose, emerald,
sky and
many others.

FINN FOAM COMPANY

Order as many cushions as you want, some of which are *not* the colours specified in the advertisement. Mention how you wish to pay for the cushions.

Extra practice 2: Requests for information, explanation and clarification

(This practice is to be used after Unit 6.2, Practices 3 and 4)

Write *one* letter:

A You are in Britain. You need to travel back to the Continent by British Rail Ferry (Dover–Ostend). You want information on times, prices, and the length of the journey. You also want to know about possible economy fares (out-of-season fares, return fares etc.). Write an appropriate letter to British Rail.

B You are studying in Britain for two years. You have a student visa for one year, which is going to run out in two months' time. Write to the Home Office, explaining your situation, and asking how you may 'regularise' your visa position (give dates, passport details etc.).

(Immigration Section,
The Home Office,
Lunar House,
Wellesley,
Croydon,
Surrey)

6.2 Test 1

Do *both* A and B:

A Below you will find an advertisement for a record shop. Write to
  the shop, ordering two of the *advertised* records; include a cheque
  in your letter; ask for a Gramophone Catalogue to be sent in the
  December of each year.

A selection from OUR NEW GERMAN IMPORTS —

BACH
Well-Tempered Clavier (complete).
Wanda Landowska, harpsichord.
RCA26.35005 .... 5 recs £17·50

BEETHOVEN
Fidelio. NBC SO/Toscanini.
RCA26.35010 .... £6·50

SHOSTAKOVITCH
First and Seventh Symphonies.
NBC SO/Toscanini.
RCA26.35105 .... £6·50

BEETHOVEN
Complete Symphonies. NBS SO/
Toscanini.
RCA26.35115 .... 6 recs £17·50

TOSCANINI
conducts Wagner. NBC SO, Trau-
bel, Melchior.
RCA26.35111 ...... 4 recs £12·50

CHERUBINI
Symphony in D, Overtures to
'Medea', 'Ali Baba' and 'Ana-
creonte' NBC SO/Toscanini.
RCA26.41311 .... £3·25

BRAHMS
3rd Symphony. NBC SO/Toscanini
RCA26.41313 .... £3·25

SIBELIUS
2nd Symphony. NBC SO/Toscanini.
RCA26.41343 .... £3·25

TCHAIKOVSKY
Manfred Symphony. NBC SO/
Toscanini.
RCA26.41366 .... £3·25

CHERUBINI
Requiem. Robert Shaw Chorus,
NBC SO/Toscanini.
RCA26.41368 .... £3·25

STRAUSS
Don Quixote. Frank Miller, NBC
SO/Toscanini.
RCA26.41369 .... £3·25

SAINT-SAENS
3rd Symphony. NBC SO/Toscanini
RCA26.41413 .... £3·25

WEBER
Clarinet Concerti. Benny Goodman,
Chicago SO/Martinon.
RCA26.41149 .... £4·50

ELIZABETH RETHBERG
Arias by Verdi, Wagner, Mozart,
Gounod etc.
RCA26.41409 .... £3·75

WEBER
Freischutz- and Jubel- Masses.
Schwann 0708/9 .... 2 recs £7·95

SCHUBERT
Lazarus (oratorio).
Schwann 3515 .... £3·95

HANDEL
St John Passion (complete).
Schwann 3515 .... £3·95

DONIZETTI
Messa di Gloria e Credo.
Schwann 3520 .... £3·95

FRANCK
Les Beatitudes (oratorio).
Schwann 4504/5 .... 2 recs £7·95

VRANICKY REICHA ZELENKA
Symphonies in honour of the French
Revolution. Prague SO/Smetacek.
Schwann 4510/11 .... 2 recs £7·95

BEETHOVEN
Organ Music. Krumbach.
Schwann 2592 .... £3·95

MOZART
Davvide Penetente and other choral
works.
Schwann 0708/9 .... 2 recs £7·95

DOMESTIC MAIL ORDERS – to 11 Great Marlborough Street London W1.
Post & Packing: 50p for 1 record, 75p for 2 or more; orders over £25 post-free.
OVERSEAS CUSTOMERS – deduct 7½% v.a.t. from prices in this
advertisement.
Despatches of £75 or more sent post-free. Please supply alternative choices
to ensure this minimum requirement. Postage for smaller orders is charged
at cost. Please ask for our Price and Special Offers lists. We cannot accept
credit cards.
**LIBRARIES, INSTITUTIONAL CUSTOMERS and
BULK EXPORTERS** supplied at discount.

Henry Stave and Company

11 Great Marlborough Street London W1 01-734 2092
Open Mon-Sat 10-6pm. 'Phone 01-4374153/5 for mail order and other enquiries
9 Dean Street Oxford Street London W1 01-437 2757
Open Mon-Fri 10-6pm, Sat 10-5pm
29 King William Street London EC4 01-283 4411
Open Mon-Fri 9-6pm

B You want to apply for *one* of the jobs below. You *understand* everything in the advertisement but you want to know more about certain things mentioned in the advertisement. Write to the appropriate person for more information about the job, and for explanations and clarifications of the advertisement.

MUSIC + DANCE CO-ORDINATOR

to organise, with an assistant, the programme of contemporary music and dance performances, workshops and talks – working as one of a small management group responsible for the overall policy and running of the Arnolfini arts complex.

University degree (or equivalent) preferred. A special interest in contemporary music with an enthusiasm and ability to put new developments into a wider context. Previous administrative experience essential.

Starting salary in range £5730 to £8114 plus generous fringe benefits. Full details from David Roe, director, 16 Quayside, Bristol BS1 4QA. Closing date 8 November.

GROW WITH US!

An opportunity has arisen for a responsible person to fill a key position in our rapidly expanding group.

We require a

MANAGER or MANAGERESS

for our Retail Home Improvement Warehouse which will open soon at

TORQUAY

Retail or general supervisory experience essential. Preferred age 25–40.

Salary of £9000, PLUS bonus of up to £1000, PLUS company car, pension scheme, telephone allowance.

We are the leading private company in our field and currently have ten Warehouses throughout the South. Our sales have grown from scratch to approaching £7 million in six years.

Please write for application form in confidence to M Robertshaw, Director
Katelise Group Limited
Winterfield Road, Paulton, Nr Bristol

Interviews will be held at Torquay.

GREAT MILLS
Warehouses & Discount Centres

6.2 Test 2

Do *both* A and B:

A *Either* Five years ago you bought the record-player shown below. You would like the player serviced. Explain what you think is wrong with it (see picture below) and ask for someone to service it.

Or You own a British-made guitar. A number of things need doing to the guitar to get it back into excellent condition. Write a letter to the makers (Aram Musical Instrument Company, Crown Lane, Ipswich, Suffolk, GB) asking them if they could repair it. Explain in detail what is wrong.

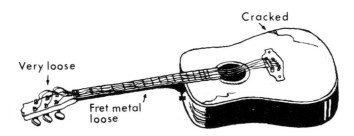

B Genesis International Bookshop, in Charing Cross Road, London WC1, who have traditionally employed foreign assistants, have promised you a job there (over the phone!) starting on the first of next month. However, you have no idea at all about what your hours of work will be, clothes you might need, what permits you might need (residence? work?) or how long you will be able to work there etc. In fact, since you don't live in London, you don't even have a clear idea of how to get there!

  Write a letter requesting the information, instructions and directions you need, based on the information above.

6.3 Letters of application

Most jobs are applied for via an application form but some, as in the advertisement in the model, demand a letter of application. As suggested in the model for this unit, applications should consist of a phrase of application including a reference to the origin of the information about the job being applied for; any inquiries you wish to make about the job; a description of your relevant experience (unless the concern offering the job ask for a curriculum vitae); a list of reasons suggesting why you ought to be considered for the job.

Adequate language notes are to be found in the Student's Book (page 121). There are four different sorts of practices in this unit: for temporary work, for full-time jobs, for educational courses, and for cultural exchanges. Students should do the practices that they feel are relevant to them; there is no progression from one to another.

Extra practice 1: Applications for temporary work

Write A *or* B below:

A
> **AUPAIR** wanted for April-September for 2 children, 6 & 8; must like children. Pocket-money by arrangement. Please apply in writing: Mrs. L. Howe, Land Road, Brixham.

Apply for this job. Include age, nationality, quality of your English, and personal details. Ask any questions you feel are relevant. Say when you would be available for an interview.

B
> **GENESIS INTERNATIONAL BOOKSHOP.** We are looking for English-speaking assistants immediately. Non-British applicants especially welcome BUT must speak English—must like books! Apply: Personnel Manager, Genesis International Bookshop, Charing Cross Road, London WC1

Apply for the job above, including the relevant personal information. Ask about hours and wages.

Extra practice 2: Applications for full-time jobs

Apply for *one* of the posts advertised below:
In your letter
mention: where you saw the advert
            why you want to apply
            qualifications
            relevant experience
            English-language ability
            work-permit problems (if non-EEC member)

ask: anything you think you need to know

WADHAM STRINGER

require a

SKILLED MECHANIC

Competitive rates of pay plus bonus together with other benefits
Come and talk to us and learn about our expanding company

Contact:
JAMES SMITH
01-752-6432

BARCLAYS BANK, Brentwood, have vacancies for Summer Auxiliary Staff. Previous banking experience essential. Good pay and conditions, with hours by arrangement.—Applicants should write giving full details please to Barclays Bank, 60 Fleet Street, Brentwood.

CASHIER WANTED to join Marion and Carol. Good conditions and pay.—Apply Mr Kirk, Southampton Road Service Station. Southampton 65971.

HAIRSTYLIST

required

Fully qualified for very busy happy salon. Excellent conditions. Wages.

**Apply Box B29911 H.E.
Newcastle**

6.3   Test 1

Write A or B, whichever is most appropriate:

A

> Are you foreign and young? We need language assistants to work with small groups for foreign language conversation.
>
> All languages needed! Temporary (min. 4 weeks) or permanent jobs available.
>
> Apply in writing to The Principal, European Language Centre, Regent St., London WC1 5YH.
>
> Give relevant personal information, and reasons why you think you're suitable.

B

> British Education Trust is offering bursaries (£2,300) for a year's education in Britain. Education or training is offered in the following subjects:
>
> Medicine/Building/Commerce/Banking Agriculture/Craft/Education.
>
> Applications should be made in writing to British Education Trust, PO Box 1138, Manchester.

6.3   Test 2

Write *either* A (application for jobs) *or* B (other applications) *or* both.

A

> # The Youth Hostels Association of England & Wales (8, St Stephen's Hill, St Albans) invites applications for assistant-wardenships at 6 hostels in Britain. Applicants may be of any nationality. Duties will include hostel maintenance, ordering supplies, cooking, accounts.
>
> # Applications should be submitted in writing.

B

> **Brandon Hall Educational Trust are organising a week's craft course at Brandon Hall (May 21st-28th) with the following options: weaving, dyeing, spinning, jewellery, pottery, enamelling, carving. Places are strictly limited; fees will be about £165 for the week.**
>
> **Please apply in writing, stating craft interests, experience, and reasons for wishing to attend the week's craft course.**
>
> **The following specialists will be resident as 'Master' craftsmen and craftswomen.:**
>
> | | |
> |---|---|
> | **Weaving:** | **James Llewellyn** |
> | **Dyeing:** | **Alicia Rainer** |
> | **Pottery:** | . . . . . . |

6.4 Giving information

There are times when one is asked to give information of various sorts to officials and companies. Since both the form and the language of these letters depend upon the original request or need, nothing useful can be stated here by way of guidance.

The criteria teachers should use to mark the practices in this unit are the effectiveness and economy of means employed to set out the information required.

6.4 Test 1

Write an appropriate letter:

You have decided to work as a nurse or medical orderly in Britain. Your future employers (Grant's Nursing Agency) have written to you:

```
Please also furnish us with a complete account of
your present and past health record:
    *   childhood illnesses
    *   serious adult illnesses
    *   any periods spent in hospital (minor or
        serious)
    *   any disabilities (minor or serious)
    *   sight
    *   hearing
    *   general state of health at present time
(This information will be kept strictly
confidential.)
```

Reply to the agency giving the information they want.

6.4   Test 2

Write either A or B:

A You have agreed to take part in a survey about 'The Family'. You
   have been asked to submit information about your immediate
   family:
   – who they are
   – ages
   – when you last saw them

   (send letter to:
   Director, Family Survey,
   Tavistock Institute,
   Tavistock Square,
   London WC2)

B You have applied to work for a period in an old people's home.
   The people who run the home have asked you to give them
   information about your
   – informal experiences of old people
   – any organised experience of working or being with old people
     you may have
   (Brent Home for the Aged, Brent, London)

6.5   Giving instructions

There are times when a foreign person will need to give instructions to
officials and companies. The forms and language used both depend
upon the context. Notes on precise language forms to be used for
giving instructions are to be found in the Student's Book (page 129).

Extra practice

Write *one* of the letters suggested below:

A You have just moved to an English-speaking country. You are
living in the country and the house is not easy to find. Your
luggage is going to be delivered by a transport firm. Using the map
below, write a letter to the firm giving precise directions and
instructions (e.g. not after 3 p.m.; go to back door) for delivery.

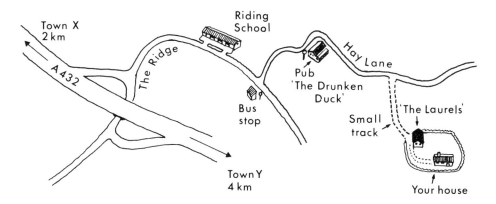

B You want to hold a party for a number of friends but don't want
the bother of doing all the food yourself. A nearby American-
owned restaurant specialises in food for parties. Write to them,
giving instructions for supplying food for a party of 20 people.

6.5 Test 1

You've been in Britain for a year, and have bought a number of
things, which include a large artificial plant and a lot of pottery. You
are now going home, and want to send your things home properly
packed.

Write to a British company (Bendells Ltd (Carriers), 40 Goodge St,
Bath) instructing them to pack up and send your things to your home
address. Give careful instructions about particular items, including
the plant and the pottery.

123

6.5 Test 2

Write a suitable letter for the situation below:

You have decided to order a rocking-chair from a British craftsman.
Send him a letter, giving precise instructions about:
— materials to be used
— rough dimensions and design
— materials for cushions and back cover
— where you would like it delivered
— an approximate delivery date

(Mr Peter Snaresbrook,
The Case,
Epping, Essex)

6.6 Letters of complaint

People write letters of complaint when they are the victims of a
mistake, or of careless, thoughtless behaviour, or administrative
inefficiency; or when they take upon themselves the task of pointing
out mistakes, thoughtlessness and inefficiency. Letters of complaint
must contain a description or report of the matter at issue, and some
form of complaint or protest. Description and report depend upon the
context. Suggestions for the language used when complaining have
been made in the language notes section on page 131 of the Student's
Book.

   Good, effective complaint letters are difficult to write. Foreign
students tend to write over-aggressive letters that would not generally
produce the apologetic or contrite response demanded. Understatement
and mild irony are often better weapons; however, even the effectiveness
of these depends upon precise situations.

Extra practice

Write *one* of the following letters:

A Write a letter to your nearest British Council office complaining
about awkward opening hours, and also poor advertising for
cultural events – you have missed two events you wanted to go to
recently.

B For the second time in a week, parcels from your own country
have arrived damaged. Write a letter of complaint to the Post
Office, describing the damage in detail.

C Write to the Principal of the educational establishment you are
studying English at, complaining about the working conditions for
students (e.g. heating / ventilation / changing rooms / facilities for
coats / furniture / noise).

6.6 Test 1

Write a *polite* letter of complaint to the manager of the students'
restaurant about some or all of the following things in the restaurant:

quality of the food
luke-warm food
service
dirty tables/plates
staff attitudes

6.6 Test 2

Write the letter suggested below:

A British record shop (DISCONO, Conduit Stret, London) have just
sent you two records. One of the records has some or all of the
following things wrong with it:
– noisy surface
– sleeve has come unglued
– only 32 minutes total playing time
– no sheet of words of songs as advertised
Write a letter of complaint to DISCONO and request that some
action be taken.

6.7 Letters of apology and explanation

Very occasionally individuals find the need to offer an apology to a
company or some form of officialdom. Such letters will consist of a
description of the issue; an apology for an action, mistake or
omission; an explanation for the action, mistake or omission; a
promise to rectify the situation (if possible). Further language help is
suggested here, beyond that offered in the Student's Book.

Description: (introductory forms)
I'm afraid I ...
I regret to say that we ...

Promises: I hope to / to be able to ...
I should/ought to be able ...

Plans: I'm coming into Troon next week so ...
I'm going to be in contact with X ...

Explanation: Owing to ...
This was due to / on account of ...
The reason for this was / has been ...

I forgot ...
mislaid ...
lost ...
misunderstood ...

In marking the practices in this unit, teachers should be sensitive to
tone: students should avoid too much self-abasement or humility – it
sounds insincere – unless the issue is an extremely serious one.

Extra practice

Write a letter appropriate for *one* of the situations described below:

A   You receive this short letter from a British Company:

```
Dear Madam
            We are sorry to inform you that our delivery team
    were unable to deliver the sofa and two armchairs ordered by
    you on Monday 8th October.  They called at 3.15 and found
    nobody in, despite the fact that 3.15 on that date was the
    time arranged by you for delivery.  Could you please confirm
    that you do wish to accept delivery of such goods and
    specify a new date and time for such
```

Write a letter of explanation and apology in response, and also specify your instructions.

B   While you were in America for a three-month stay you rented an apartment. You have returned to your own country now. You have just had a short letter from the owner of the apartment asking for the set of keys that you should have returned before you left. Reply to the owner's letter.

6.7   Test 1

Write *one* of the letters suggested below:

A   A British tour operator asked you to write a report in England on a holiday you took with them (they were going to pay you a small fee for this). You have not sent your report yet, so write a letter apologising for and explaining the delay.

B   You were invited to attend an interview for a job in an American-owned hotel. You did not turn up for this interview. Write a letter apologising for this and explain why you failed to go. Request another interview.

6.7 Test 2

Write *one* of the letters suggested below:

A You went for an interview for a job which involved looking after ski-chalets in Switzerland for British winter tourists. At the interview you were accepted for the job, and told the holiday company you would make your decision within three days. It is now seven days later, and the company have just written to you asking you for a decision one way or the other. Write a letter apologising for your delay and offering explanations.

B Write a letter to Bournemouth Central Library after you discover that you have accidently taken three of their library books home with you to your own country.

Section 7 Presenting facts, ideas and opinions

Introduction

On the whole most foreign users of English do not need to develop very great competence in writing the text-types offered in this section, even though within the category of personal writing people will inevitably wish to present facts or present and express ideas and opinions. Fortunately then, less time appears to be spent in the modern EFL classroom on the production of complete essays, reports and summaries than was previously the case. Professional interest or academic requirements will be the main reason for students choosing to work on this section.

All the units in this section make use of particular language functions: describing, narrating, comparing, exemplifying, generalising, hypothesising, summarising, offering conclusions, evaluating. It is not possible to suggest a complete list of language items that a writer needs for these units. However, one may suppose that other general textual skills are pre-eminently important; these are the skills involved in actually putting together expository text:

sequencing   (using sequencing and itemising markers)
linking   (semantically or formally by
               Conjuncts e.g. Nevertheless, . . . In addition, . . .
               Conjunctions e.g. When . . . Although . . . Because . . .)
referencing   (use of substitution devices for
               Noun phrases e.g. I like ice cream. Can I have <u>one</u>?
               Adverbials e.g. We are going to York. We'll see you <u>there</u>.
               Predicate and Predication e.g. She drives. I think Anna <u>does</u> too.
               Sentence/Clause: anaphora e.g. They like the sea. <u>That's</u> why they
                  come every year; cataphora e.g. <u>Here</u> is the news: in Rome today . . .)
refining propositions   (by the use of qualifying and modifying devices, participle
                  relatives etc.)

A further skill may be suggested, which is that concerning a writer's ability to indicate his own relation to what is being written:

disjuncts (or comment clauses) Frankly, . . . Without hesitation, . . . Briefly, . . .
comment phrases   It would be foolish to suggest that . . . I would hope that . . .

Of the five units in the section, the last four are text-types in themselves. Unit 7.1 is concerned with the paragraph, which all the other units depend upon, and so may be seen as a necessary preparation for all of them.

7.1 Paragraph writing

The ability to write clear, coherent, and cohesive paragraphs is a writing skill that is fundamental to all expository writing (and thus may be seen as a pre-requisite to successful writing in the other units in this section).

A complete text may consist of a single paragraph, but on the whole paragraphs usually belong to a larger text-type such as an essay or a report. Since, however, paragraphs are regarded as complete at the micro-textual level it is valuable to treat the writing of them as a whole activity.

As whole texts, paragraphs have a single theme or topic, and almost inevitably have one complete statement around which the paragraph is organised. The paragraph is therefore a powerful way of presenting facts, ideas or opinions.

As has been suggested in M. L. Imhoof and H. Hudson's excellent book *From Paragraph to Essay* (Longman 1975) the paragraph, like the essay, may be developed in a number of ways: by exemplification, by contrast and comparison, by definition, by classification, by reference to space or to time, by cause and effect relations and by generalisation.

To write successful and convincing paragraphs (and thus any expository language) students will need to develop the ability to:

present factual or theoretical ideas
support and add to propositions   Moreover, ... In addition, ...
                                     Further, ...

present counter-propositions   On the other hand, ... In contrast, ...

offer evidence and illustration   For example/instance ... Such as ...
                                     An illustration of this would be ...

summarise, generalise, and   All in all, ... To sum up ... In summary,
   conclude   ... Consequently, we can suggest ...

The exercises in this book have been designed to help students recognise that paragraphs *are* units of textual meaning by identifying themes and main sentences; and secondly, to learn to use, in controlled fashion, the linguistic devices by which writers in English present, add to, counter, illustrate, exemplify, generalise about, summarise, and offer conclusions about facts and ideas.

7.1 Exercises 1

Read through each of the paragraphs below and for each one
(a) write down very briefly what the paragraph is about; (b) find a
main sentence for the paragraph – if there is one.

1 But the British distaste for trade had deeper roots than these institutional
structures: already by the mid-nineteenth century the first enthusiasm for
industrial progress was leading to a relapse into disillusion, rural nostalgia
and the search for an unspoilt old England. The early Dickens, excited by
modern manufacture, gave way to the sceptical Dickens of *Hard Times*
and *Our Mutual Friend*. The rugged enterprise of early northern engineers
and mechanics gave way to the respectability and gentrification of the
professions and institutes. The sons of industrialists were cleansed of trade
and commercial ambition by the burgeoning public schools, and retreated
into country estates.
(Anthony Sampson *The Changing Anatomy of Britain*)

2 Whatever the underlying social causes, for two decades after the Second
World War British companies were sitting ducks for the predators – sitting
on valuable assets, with weak managers and passive shareholders. The old
family brewers, shop-owners or ship-owners strikingly demonstrated the
British lack of interest in business. A handful of Jewish entrepreneurs –
including Charles Clore, Isaac Wolfson, Max Joseph, Jack Cotton and
Max Rayne – bought up their companies and properties cheaply and
developed them to rapidly push up their profits and share prices. Within
ten years the pattern of ownership had already drastically changed.
(Anthony Sampson *The Changing Anatomy of Britain*)

3 Everything which made the Indian alien in the society gave him strength.
His alienness insulated him from the black–white struggle. He was
taboo-ridden as no other person on the island: he had complicated rules
about food and about what was unclean. His religion gave him values
which were not the white values of the rest of the community, and
preserved him from self-contempt; he never lost pride in his origins. More
important than religion was his family organisation, an enclosing self-
sufficient world absorbed with its quarrels and jealousies, as difficult for
the outsider to penetrate as for one of its members to escape. It protected
and imprisoned, a static world, awaiting decay.
(V. S. Naipaul *The Middle Passage*)

4 Every country has imposed its own national characteristics on the new
medium, which has always been more circumscribed and regulated than
newspapers, books or films; and British television soon began to reflect the
traditions of its people. It could claim to provide the best programmes in
the world in terms of democratic argument, serious documentaries and
above all drama; it provided a new kind of stage for the British theatrical
tradition which had already lasted four centuries. It brought great acting,
Olympic sport, opera and exploration into millions of homes which would
never otherwise have seen them, without the debasement of taste and the
extreme intrusions of advertising on the American screens; and it could

appeal across classes, whether with comedy series or with political
documentaries, as newspapers had never done.
(Anthony Sampson *The Changing Anatomy of Britain*)

5 I had never liked the sugarcane fields. Flat, treeless and hot, they stood for
everything I had hated about the tropics and the West Indies. 'Cane Is
Bitter' is the title of a story by Samuel Selvon and might well be the
epigraph of a history of the Caribbean. It is a brutal plant, tall and
grass-like, with rough razor-edged blades. I knew it was the basis of the
economy, but I preferred trees and shade. Now, in the uneven land of
central and south Trinidad, I saw that even sugarcane could be beautiful.
On the plains just before crop-time, you drive through it. Walls of grass
either side; but in rolling country you can look down on a hillside covered
with tall sugarcane in arrow: steel-blue plumes dancing above a grey–
green carpet, grey–green because each long blade curves back on itself,
revealing its paler underside.
(V. S. Naipaul *The Middle Passage*)

6 Anger is another strong, potentially disruptive emotion that must be
maturely managed. Differences among those with whom one works are
inevitable and must be settled without violence or lasting scars. Anger
should never be expressed thoughtlessly just for venting it. It may give
temporary cathartic relief, but the damage done to work relationships can
be permanent and irrevocable. The immediate pleasure of emotional
discharge must be passed up in favour of long-term considerations. That is
not to say that anger should never be expressed, but that much thought
should be given to the consequences. Giving voice to hostility at the
correct time can affect those toward whom it is directed and thus benefit a
woman at the same time as that tension is reduced.
(William Appleton *Fathers and Daughters*)

7 A fully realized adult woman does not depend on others for her
self-esteem. In fact, she expects others to *perceive* her value, not to create
it. She does not desire approval indiscriminately or for its own sake, but
only if it is expressed because of attributes she respects in herself. She is not
so much concerned with what someone thinks of her as with what *she*
thinks of him or her. Unlike a child stuck with parents, family, or teachers,
she picks her own intimates according to standards she creates.
(William Appleton *Fathers and Daughters*)

Exercises 2

You should do these exercises if you find you are having difficulty
writing coherent logical paragraphs after doing Practice 1.

   These two exercises should help you to write paragraphs that
develop in a clear controlled way.

1   PARAGRAPH SKELETONS

Write four sentences as instructed below on *boots*. These four sentences
put together should give you the skeleton of a paragraph on boots.
a) Say what a boot is.
b) Say who wears boots (farmers/children/women/fishermen).
c) Say why people wear boots (keep dry/fashion).
d) Make a statement about yourself and boots.

Now write another skeleton of three sentences on *income tax*.
a) Give a definition of income tax.
b) State how tax is collected (different ways?).
c) Give a general idea about how people feel about income tax.

Now write a third skeleton of four sentences about *vegetarianism*.
a) State simply what vegetarianism is.
b) Moral reasons for vegetarianism.
c) Health reasons for vegetarianism.
d) Your attitude to vegetarianism.

2   DEVELOPING A PARAGRAPH

In this exercise you should develop your skeleton, and then add things
to the basic sentences.

   Write a three-sentence skeleton about make-up. These are your
main sentences.
1 Describe briefly what make-up is.
2 Say who generally wears make-up.
3 Offer an explanation of why people wear make-up.

Now expand your skeleton in the following ways:

1 main sentence + 1a – different parts of the body applied to
                       1b – simple, subtle make-up compared to 'heavy' make-up

2 main sentence + 2a – use in the theatre and television
                       2b – use in police work and detection

3 main sentence + 3a – an example of making oneself more beautiful
                       3b – an example of hiding a defect or something ugly
                       3c – an example of using make-up to change character

4 Offer your own opinion on the use of make-up.

Extra practice 1

This practice should be used after Unit 7.1, Practices 1 and 2 in the Student's Book.

Use the main sentences below as a basis for your paragraph-writing. Choose *two*. Concentrate upon making your writing accurate and clear.

A Write a 90–100 word paragraph *beginning* with the main sentence:
'The British attitude towards food is very different from the attitudes in my own country . . . '

B Write a 90–100 word paragraph *ending* with the main sentence:
'. . . Altogether I think that this is a book that everyone should read.'

C Write a 90–100 word paragraph *containing* the sentence:
'My grandfather / grandmother is / was very easy / difficult to get on with.'

D Write a clear paragraph *beginning* with the main sentence:
'There are no justifications for any country possessing nuclear weapons.'
or
'There are a number of reasons to justify a country possessing nuclear weapons.'

Extra practice 2

This gives more free paragraph-writing practice, and should be used after Unit 7.1, Practices 3 and 4.
N.B. Your paragraph should be clearly based on one idea, perhaps stated somewhere in the paragraph by a main sentence.

Choose *one* of the following:

A Write a 100–120 word paragraph on *Power*.

B Write a 90–100 word paragraph on *Being blind*.

C Write a paragraph on *Weddings*.

7.1 Test 1

Write *both* paragraphs below:

A Write a 100 word paragraph beginning 'There are a number of
advantages/disadvantages in allowing cars into the centre of cities.'

B Write a paragraph on *one* of the following subjects:
i) Leaving the parental home.
ii) Returning to the parental home for visits.

7.1 Test 2

Write *both* paragraphs below:

A Write a 100 word paragraph ending '... These are only some of
the problems likely to arise in mixed marriages.'

B Write a paragraph on *one* of the following subjects:
i) Examination nerves.
ii) Using the telephone.

7.2   Letters to newspapers

As suggested in the model (Student's Book page 142), people write
letters to newspapers in order to comment on current affairs in
general, or on previous items in the newspaper; to support or argue
against views expressed or comments made in the newspaper; to
complain about or praise something.

As far as the rhetorical conventions used in letters to newspapers
are concerned, they are no different to those used for letters to
officials or companies; the address form is invariably 'Dear Sir'
although newspapers often omit such details, when printing letters
written to them.

As for the language necessary for the writing of letters to
newspapers, reference should be made to the introduction to this
section and to the remarks made in the introduction to Unit 7.1.
However, students should learn how to refer to ideas or articles in
previous editions of the newspaper or magazine in the following
ways:

The article on/about ... which appeared in ...	of (date) ... on (date) ...
The views/ideas/opinions expressed in the article published ...	
The report which appeared in the ... of/on ...	claimed/stated ... suggested/implied ...

Here are some excerpted examples of the way those who write to
newspapers or magazines actually refer to the theme of their letters:

'... Having been involved in local authority attempts to provide sites for
Gypsies for much of the last six years, I cannot allow Jesse Heron's eloquent
but one-sided article (Guardian, September 8) to pass without comment ...'

'Sir – Anthony Tucker's article (September 11) on the Dangerous Wild
Animals Act served a useful purpose in drawing people's attention ...'

'... Sir, I was interested to see the reference in Guardian Diary (September
11) to "the Guardian's reproductive processes" ...'

'... An article in the Guardian on September 11th discusses the extinction of
dinosaurs 65 million years ago ...'

'Sir – In your leader on the Liberal Party debate you quote Mr ...'

'Mrs Bagshaw's letter about milk bottles in the washing machine reminded
me of a similar experience. Having loaded and switched on ...'

'... You are right in your recent "COMMENT" to call for the abolition of
...'

'... Mrs E. H. ROYLE (Letters) is a little premature in expecting to buy
home-grown potatoes. As all good gardeners know ...'

136

Extra practice

Write *two* of the letters to newspapers suggested below.

A Write a letter to a national British newspaper commenting (not necessarily complaining) on the British attitude to (i) pets or (ii) Sunday.

B You quite like living in Britain, but you are very upset by the standard of hot drinks served in restaurants and coffee bars. Write a letter to the local paper complaining about this, giving some details; make some recommendations.

C Read the article below and write a letter commenting on it, to the national newspaper of your choice:

DOG-LOVER Herbert Johns was jailed for five days yesterday after refusing to pay fines imposed for walking his pet labrador Ricky in a park.

As his sentence was announced by magistrates in his home town of Burnley, 57-year-old Johns declared: 'I'll go on hunger strike if you send me to prison. I don't intend to pay the fines. I can't in conscience do so.'

He had failed to pay fines imposed for contravening Burnley's controversial by-law banning dogs from local parks. Johns broke the by-law four times and was fined £5 for each offence but his wife had paid off £4 without his knowledge.

D Read the article below and write a letter to the editor of a national newspaper on the subject.

Farms

TALKS over a farmworkers' pay claim for what amounts to a 125 per cent. increase, ended in deadlock last night.

The farm workers, who staged a demonstration in London yesterday, want an increase from £60 to £100 on their minimum weekly wage, a cut from the basic 40 hours a week to 35 hours and other improvements.

Last night, however, farmer members of the Agricultural Wages Board refused to improve their offer of a package inside the 5 per cent. guideline which would include higher overtime pay and premiums for skill and experience.

The talks resume on Friday.

137

7.2 Test 1

Write *one* of the letters below (write a minimum of 150 words):

A In the time you have spent in Britain you have watched quite a lot of British television. There may be things you admire and/or things you would like to criticise about the quality and content of British television. Write a letter to a national newspaper about it.

B You see the following text in a magazine. It is being used to help sell whisky. Write a letter to the editor of the magazine, commenting on the text.

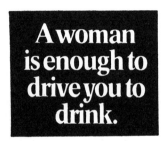

C After you have read the letter below entitled 'Mis-spent youth?' you feel that you have a number of opinions on the subject. Write a letter to the newspaper in response – you may agree, disagree or simply add to the arguments.

Mis-spent youth?

DR RHODES BOYSON'S suggestion that university students should pay back money spent on their further education fills me with horror.

This terrible imposition would come at the most vulnerable time of a graduate's life—at the start of a career, with perhaps a wife and child to support.

When are we going to recognise, without envy, that our university students are an important part of our future prosperity?

(Mrs) V. LLOYD-JONES,
Cwmbran, Gwent.

7.2   Test 2

Write *one* of the letters below (write a minimum of 150 words):

A You have been learning English for some years now, and also
   listening to British, American, Canadian etc. people speak it. Write
   a letter to the Editor, *Modern English Teacher*, MEP, PO Box 129,
   Oxford OX2 8JU, about some aspects of English you find
   interesting, or strange, or difficult to understand.

B Write a letter to the newspaper commenting on the extract below,
   which appeared in their paper.

IT'S a woman's life in the British Army.

Service chiefs are launching a campaign to woo girls to join up.

They want to double the number of women serving with the Army. And more Navy and RAF jobs will go to women, too.

C You have just read the letter below and have some opinions on the
   subject. Write a letter to the newspaper in response.

Check out labels

I HAVE unknowingly, bought in Britain clothes pegs from Russia, sweets from Cuba, grease-proof paper from Norway, a photo album from Japan and a hair spray from America.

I am furious at myself — and the country—for allowing these to be imported when we should be making and selling them ourselves. Look for the labels !

J. H. FAWCETT,
Sheffield, S. Yorkshire.

7.3 Summary reports

Notes on why people may need to write summaries, and the uses that
people have for summaries are suggested on page 148 of the Student's
Book. It is important to remember that successful summary writing
depends upon two separate skills: the ability to *read* with
understanding and focus, and the ability to *write* down what one has
read in a shorter, more streamlined form without destroying the sense
or the intentions of the original. This sort of writing is difficult to do
well in a formal sense (and has remained a much-hated item in
native-speaker language examinations) but it is a kind of writing that
occurs more often than people generally realise. A friend writing to
another and offering an account of a book that he has just read is
providing a summary to his addressee.

Since the writing of summary reports depends upon a clear
understanding of the original text (written or spoken) there is a need
for accurate note-taking. Advice and illustrations of note-taking for
summary purposes are offered with the models on page 149 of the
Student's Book.

Nothing can be said about the textual form or language employed
by summaries since this depends entirely on the form and language of
the original. However, the writing of summary reports based on
speech does have to obey the linguistic rules for reported speech in
English. Practice in reporting speech is given in Unit 5.4, where the
exercises may be useful.

Model summaries are provided in the Key, page 167.

Extra practice 1

Sometimes you need to write quick summaries of official documents –
especially in informal transmission of information i.e. personal letters
etc. The two items below are designed to practise this:

Do *both* A and B:

A Here is an official
account of what you
must pay income tax
on in Britain. Read it
very carefully, and
then write a short
summary of what you
have to put onto the
tax form.

Income : Year ended 5 April

Earnings

1   Main employment
You do not have to enter details or pay from your own full-time
employment. Your employer supplies this information to the
Inspector.

2   Wife's employment
Enter the name and address of your wife's employer and her
works number. Enter the total earnings less any superannuation
contribution deducted by her employer in calculating her pay
for tax purposes but before any other deductions.

3   All other earnings
You must enter all your other earnings, wherever they come
from. You must include all your and your wife's casual and
spare-time earnings including earnings as an agency worker.

Say briefly the type of work done and give the names and
addresses of all the people for whom you worked. Enter the total
amount earned before deductions.

4   Tips and other incidental receipts
The total amount of tips and incidental receipts from ALL
SOURCES (including your main employment), the value of any
goods or earnings in kind should be entered here.

If your employer (or someone else) provides by reason of your
employment:

● medical insurance or vouchers exchangeable for goods,
services or money enter the expense incurred by your
employer (or the other person)

● living accommodation, enter the address, rent payable and
gross value for rating.

B Below are four short descriptions of books. Write a *sentence*
summary of each book, keeping the basic ideas but omitting mere
detail.

AIRSHIPWRECK
Len Deighton & Arnold Schwartzman
An astonishing story of simple pioneering faith which
gave us the brief but great age of airships.
Magnificently illustrated with almost 100 rare
photographs, the book also recalls with humour and
pathos some of the most colourful and dramatic yet
least-known incidents in the history of flying.
Cape £4.95

AVIATION:
AN ILLUSTRATED HISTORY
Christopher Chant
Throughout this fascinating book, topics of technical
or social interest are carefully explained through
picture essays, and lavish full-colour drawings of
several of the world's greatest aircraft show off the
technical features that made them famous: 100
colour photographs and 400 in black-and-white. 304
pages. *Orbis £7.95*

CATHEDRALS IN BRITAIN & IRELAND
William Anderson & Clive Hicks
Describes the sixty-two cathedrals existing before the
Reformation, with special attention to their historical
associations and individual settings. Magnificent
photographs taken by Clive Hicks (a practising
architect) accompany each description.
Macdonald & Jane's £5.95

THE HISTORY OF SHIPS
Peter Kemp
The full grandeur of this absorbing subject is captured
in more than 250 magnificent photographs, while
individual two-page sections are devoted to topics of
special interest in each period, such as navigation or
the development of the Dreadnought.

Extra practice 2

Sometimes you need to write concise summaries of official
information or commercial material – especially in informal
transmission of information in personal letters etc.

Do *both* A and B:

A Here is some
   advertising information
   about flowers. Read it
   very carefully, and then
   write two sentences
   summarising the
   information about each
   flower.

TALL FLOWERING GLADIOLI

Ref.No.G47 SUPER MIXTURE OF TALL FLOWERING GLADIOLI

A bargain offer of 8/10cm Gladioli supplied in a well balanced mixture of
colours. They are a very good buy if you are looking for something at a
reasonable price that will provide clumps of colour all around your
garden during the summer of '85. They are also useful if you are looking
for something decorative for the house.

25 for **95p** 50 for **£1.70** 100 for **£3.05** 250 for **£7.15**

BARGAIN OFFER OF MIXED GLADIOLI

Ref.No.G48 BEAUTIFUL MIXED BUTTERFLY GLADIOLI (8/10cms)

Their very name conjures up thoughts of a bloom that is colourful,
delicate and strikingly beautiful and indeed that is exactly what Butterfly
Gladioli are. They are shorter than the normal large flowering Gladioli so
this makes them ideal to use as a foil against their taller flowering cousins.
Their exquisitely shaped florets, each one finished off with delicate ruffles
on the edge of the petals make these blooms an ideal subject for the
flower arranger. Supplied in a mixture of eye-catching colours.

25 for **£1.85** 50 for **£3.35** 100 for **£5.90** 250 for **£13.85**

B Below is an announcement about study courses. Summarise the
   basic information in the announcement omitting unnecessary
   detail.

PROFESSIONALISATION

The first of a series of five courses on various
aspects of arts promotion for full-time and
voluntary administrators will be held from 21-23
March. In conjunction with the Centre for Arts
and Related Studies of the City University, and
with financial assistance from the Arts Council of
Great Britain, these courses are being organised
by South West Arts as part of a scheme to help
arts organisations by bringing about greater professional expertise.

This first weekend (Friday evening to
Sunday lunchtime) will be devoted to *Programming and Budgeting.* It will cover aspects of
programming, budgetary control, applying for
grants, timetabling tactics and related topics.

The main guest lecturer will be John Pick,
Director of Arts Administration Studies at the
university.

Future courses will be on *Community
Theatre and Sharing* (April 11-13), *Avoiding
Disasters* (May 2-4), *Selling Yourself — Raising
Cash* (May 23-25) and *Selling Yourself — Image*
(June 13-15). It is hoped that costs for
participants will be very low. Venues in each case
will be announced in the next issue of this news-
paper. Anyone who has not already contacted
South West Arts and who wishes to be included
on any of the courses should contact John de la
Cour at South West Arts as soon as possible.
Numbers will be limited to 35 on each course
(apart from that on *Community Theatre and
Sharing*).

Extra practice 3

This practice is intended to help you summarise speeches and discussions.

Do *both* A and B:

A After reading about this dancer, Patricia Ruanne, talking about her life as a dancer, write a summary of what she says as part of a letter to a friend you know is interested in dancing.

PR: I'll dance as long as I'm able to, both physically and mentally; until there is a clear loss of strength and credibility. And when the time comes I hope people won't pussyfoot around, but will tell me honestly. No, it isn't a traumatic thought because I know it isn't going to happen yet. Not if I've got any control over my work: I won't let it happen yet. Maybe I've got eight years, until I'm 45.

I won't turn my back on the world of dance anyway. What else can I do? Serve behind Harrods counter perhaps? I'd be too old to start retraining for a new career. Anyway, that's hard when you have devoted yourself to ballet since the age of seven. I'd miss it all too much.

So that I can work longer I've already begun learning character roles and last autumn I did Carabosse in Sleeping Beauty when I was on tour in Manchester and Bristol ... you can't wait until you can no longer do ballerina roles. Character work is not that easy: a different technique is needed to command the stage and handle all those frocks and wigs.

There will be no angst when the time comes and I find myself doing the nurse or Lady Capulet instead of Juliet. There's no shame if you are good at it. Look at the Russian character dancers, they are astonishing. You either instinctively understand the value of character work or you don't. The majority of dancers wouldn't want it — they think it is too boring.

B You witnessed a road accident between a cyclist and a motorist and the police have asked you to submit a short report. The report includes a summary of this conversation between the motorist and cyclist after the accident – that you were close enough to hear.

Motorist: Um ... are you all right ... anything broken do you think ... ?

Cyclist: My left leg feels very numb ... no thanks to you – you drove right into me from behind.

Motorist: What! ... you came to a dead halt in the middle of the road and then just turned right ... I couldn't avoid hitting you ... why didn't you signal properly?

Cyclist: I did signal properly ... I was waiting in the middle of the road for quite a long time so I could turn right ... I was waiting for the stream of traffic to stop going the other way ... you must be one of those motorists who don't ever see people on bikes ... we don't have flashing lights, you know, we use our hands!

Motorist: Well, I didn't see you until you suddenly stopped bang in front of me ... you'd better learn to make better hand signals ...

7.3 Test 1

Do *both* A and B:

A Read the article entitled 'Garlic cure supported'. Take notes, and summarise the experiments with garlic and the conclusions that medical researchers have come to.

Garlic cure supported

From UPI in Bonn

West German researchers have a solution to cholesterol clogged blood vessels. It is garlic.

Old wives have for centuries claimed that garlic cures many ills — from snake bites to toothache. Now, according to Professor Hans Reuter, of Cologne, there is proof that garlic helps to clear the fat accumulating in the blood vessels of those who eat rich food, so reducing the danger of heart attacks.

Tests showed that volunteers fed on butter containing 50 grams of garlic oil had a cholesterol level considerably lower than that of a control group fed on butter without garlic.

In another experiment, patients ate three grams of raw garlic a day. After four weeks their cholesterol level fell markedly.

According to Professor Reuter, garlic not only drives out unwanted fats in blood. Tests indicated that the herb also kills other bacteria, among them those causing diphtheria and tuberculosis.

Professor Reuter said garlic was in some cases more effective than penicillin.

To get the full benefit, you must use fresh garlic. Garlic powder won't work any medicinal miracles, since the plant loses its healing properties when processed.

B Read the information about HMS Bristol (provided in a brochure produced by the Directorate of Public Relations, Royal Navy) and summarise the basic facts about the ship.

A home for the men

HMS BRISTOL, when at sea or away from her base port, is home for 29 officers and 378 ratings. She can be likened to a small town whose inhabitants carry out all the normal domestic and town chores as well as doing their daily work. Further, this town may move rapidly from the tropics to the Arctic.

Manpower is a very expensive commodity in a warship. Every member of the crew is a skilled, highly trained man, who, if he is to be economically used, must be properly managed and given every possible mechanical aid to carry out his ship upkeep duties. He also requires living conditions which are as comfortable and up to date as it is possible to provide in a fighting unit where so much space is demanded by weapons, machinery and stores.

Every effort has been made in the BRISTOL to see that these ideals have been met. She is not the first ship to have bunks, vacuum cleaners, airconditioning, laundry, NAAFI shop and a modern cafeteria — to name a few facilities — but she was among the first to have her interior decor chosen by a firm of consultants and to have her own TV studio and cameras. Points like these typify the thought and money which has been spent in making her comfortable and easy to run, as well as being a powerful fighting ship.

7.3   Test 2

Do *both* A and B:

SUMMARY OF IDEAS

A Below, Michael Foot, Leader of the Labour Party at the time (6th December, 1982), discusses Democratic Socialism during the period 1940–5. Summarise his ideas.

The best example that I've seen of Democratic Socialism operating in this country was during the Second World War. Then we ran Britain highly efficiently, got everybody into a job. It wasn't so difficult then to employ people who were disabled and in difficulties and all the rest of it. We wanted to use all their efforts, and we found the money to do it. We also produced, I would have thought, probably more than any other country including Germany. We mobilised better. The conscription of labour was only a very small element of it. We also did what I think we ought to do on a far greater scale now, looking after the people who are worst hit. In the war, instead of saying because (the country) is in extreme circumstances you've got to cut the pay of the people who are worst off, they did the opposite. They increased the pensions, the social security. It was a democratic society with a common aim in which many of the class barriers were being broken down. Many of us thought we would never return to a society in which class barriers were rebuilt. Many of them have been. And many of those class barriers are the very things which have injured the community since.

SUMMARY OF INFORMATION

B Summarise this newspaper report about how Mrs Linda Jenkins lost a lot of weight.

Pounds to the good

THE SLIMMING of "Big John and his Linda" paid a £1,000 dividend yesterday when the couple won a Slimmer of the Year contest

Later Mrs Linda Jenkins, a 27-year-old mother of two, and her husband John, of Northfield, Birmingham, revealed the "secret recipe" which within six months reduced their weights by 4 stones and 7 stones. 3 lbs respectively from their 12 stones, 8 lbs and 20 stones.

It was plain, old-fashioned dieting, they said. Out went toast dripping with butter and mounds of meat with roast potatoes, as well as John's four to five pints of beer a day, followed by curry. And in came liver, fish and chicken and lots of boiled vegetables.

And what was the most exciting difference in their lives? "How much easier our love life is," said Linda.

7.4 Personal and factual reports

Clear notes on the uses and purposes of reports are included in the Student's Book page 155. Most students who choose to work on this unit will be those who perceive a present or future professional need to produce written reports in English.

Reports contain two main features, but may contain additional parts, as suggested below:

i)   description and report | of people, places, institutions, habits, traditions
of events, series of events, human activities

(The units in Sections 4 and 5 may be very useful here.)

ii) evaluation | commendation and praise
criticism and blame
offering assessment of worth or value

In addition:

iii) recommendations   suggestions and
advice   I'd | recommend | that ...
suggest

I'd | recommend | people to ...
advise

My| suggestion | would be to ...
advice
warnings   I'd like to offer a warning ...

Extra practice 1

This practice should follow Practices 1 and 2 in the Student's Book.
Write *one* item from A and *one* item from B:

A REPORTS ON FACILITIES

Write a report for foreign students coming to your country about
the facilities available for (a) buying books
(b) borrowing books and (c) buying stationery (mention the
approximate costs of paper and writing implements).
or
Write an account of the cinemas and theatres in your town/city/
district or for a part of Britain. Go into detail about types of plays
and films shown at each theatre or cinema, frequency of
performances, size of auditoriums, prices, and audiences.

B REPORTS ON PEOPLE

Write a report on a *doctor* or a *dentist* whose patient you were
once or still are. This will involve both a personal and a
professional evaluation.
or
Think of a salesperson you know and write a critical assessment of
them as a salesperson.
or
The people you are selling your flat or house to have asked you to
write a report on the next-door neighbours – as neighbours. Do so.

Extra practice 2

This practice should follow Practices 3 and 4 in the Student's Book.
Write *one* item from A and *one* item from B.

A REPORTS OF EVENTS

Write a critical review of a concert you recently went to or saw on
television (classical/jazz/pop/folk/blues).
or
You recently went to a wedding in your country. Write a report of
the event for English or American friends, so that they have a clear
idea of the nature of the event.
or
Write a report on a recent or well-remembered protest-meeting
that you have been in (anti-nuclear weapons, anti-nuclear power,
anti-hunting, anti-vivisectionist, etc. ...).

B REPORTS ON COURSES, PROJECTS, JOBS

Write a report on a period of voluntary work you've done (e.g.
with old people, children, or the handicapped).
or
Write a report on a period of training you've done for any sport
you play or have played in the past. Include details of frequency,
variety, intensity, and difficulty. Indicate the results and success of
training.
or
You have done a first-aid training course at some time. Write a
report on this course, including details of course contents, the way
the course was run, and the success of the course from your point
of view.

7.4   Test 1

Write *one* item from A and *one* from B:

A Write a report on the general comfort and facilities available at the
   house or flat where you are living.
   or
   Write a report describing the leisure facilities in your home town,
   city or village – commenting also on their quality.

B Write a personal account of a film or TV play you've seen recently.
   or
   Write an evaluative report on your last period of education in your
   country.

7.4   Test 2

Write *one* item from A and *one* from B:

A A friend is coming to live in your town or city. She is a great walker
   and climber. Write a report on the walks and climbs available in
   the countryside around your home.
   or
   Write a critical report on the food served on aeroplanes, on trains
   and at railway stations in,
   i)   your country;
   ii) in another country.

B Write a report on the last long journey or trip you took. Comment
   on the speed, comfort, efficiency and pleasure of the journey.
   or
   Write a personal report on a game of sport you have watched
   recently.
   or
   Write an evaluative report on the way you were served in the last
   three shops you went into.

7.5 Essay-writing

Students preparing for external language examinations need to be able to write essays. However this text-type is not one that many other foreign students will need to develop. It has two main uses: an academic use for foreign students studying at university or in teacher-training; a professional use in academic papers, journalism, or the writing of professional papers.

All essay-type writing tends to break down into three identifiable parts: an introductory exposition; argument; summary and conclusions. As suggested in the Student's Book page 160, an essay-writer should be able to present an argument, idea or opinion, present a counter- or contrasting argument or idea, illustrate and exemplify ideas and arguments by presenting facts, evidence, analogies, offer factual or evaluative comments on opinions and arguments, and draw conclusions about and summarise ideas and arguments.

Some stylistic advice can be offered to the foreign student writing an essay in English, and the following are habits which are best avoided:

using very short sentences   (sounds aggressive, unsophisticated)
using very short paragraphs   (over-emphatic; argument by assertion rather than by progression of illustrated ideas)
using rhetorical questions to excess   (has an emotive rather than rational effect on reader)
using irrelevant personal examples or illustrations   (dangers of generalising – and being seen to – from personal experience alone)
using no examples or illustrations   (mere assertion)
using very long sentences   (difficult for reader to follow)
using very long paragraphs   (can be difficult to follow)

The ability to develop a text clearly and consistently is very important in this sort of writing, and the following skills should be part of a student's repertoire:

i)   linking   (cf Student's Book page 160, and Model text and Linking notes)
ii) sequencing   (letting the reader know where you are and where you are going. 'There are three ... The first is ... Secondly, ... , etc.)
iii) referencing   (ensuring that any pro-form word is not ambiguous in its reference, particularly in the use of *it* and *this*)

The writer should also know what linguistic devices to use in order to announce the following:

examples and   (for instance, for example, such as,
  illustrations   as in the case of . . .)

generalisations   (from this, it follows . . .
  and summaries   all in all, . . . when looked at as a whole, . . .)

quotations (as reported in . . . as X wrote/suggested . . .)

Key to exercises 🔑

3.1 Writing telegrams and telexes

Exercise 1
a) Get me half a pound of potatoes and two lemons.
b) I'm leaving London immediately; I'll be back on Monday.
c) Jack has gone! Where has he gone?
d) I've bought a camera; it takes good pictures.
e) My father is sick so I can't make your wedding.

Exercise 2
There may be versions which differ slightly from the ones given here.
a) Raining (here) now.
b) Mary can't come Saturday.
c) Weather lovely.
d) *No shorter version possible.*
e) Key at home on table by window.
f) Sue not going Italy – in love with Austrian (boy).
g) Get money needed from Harry.
h) No Joe? Why not? / Why no Joe?
i) Sister not returning yet – fortnight maybe?
j) Richard loves me – married soon.

Exercise 3
A number of correct versions are acceptable here.
a) Harry's family (were) late.
b) Everyone (here) happy (here).
c) He drinks a lot (of alcohol).

3.3 Writing instructions

Exercise 1 There may be alternative correct sentences.
a) Water young plants in order to keep them alive.
b) Add fertilisers to help growth.
c) To encourage strong growth, mow the grass regularly.
d) Take off dead flower-heads in order to encourage new buds to flower.

Exercise 2
a) Cut the wood in half by means of a saw.
b) Measure the wood with a ruler.
c) Tighten the screws with a screwdriver.
d) Make holes in the wood by using a drill.
e) Remove the rough edges by means of a plane.
f) Polish the finished object by applying bees wax and rubbing vigorously.
g) Attach handles by using glue and screws.

Exercise 3 Other versions may be equally acceptable.
a) First, wet hair thoroughly.
Then, undo shampoo bottle and apply shampoo.
Next, rub in shampoo.
After that, rinse hair in clean water.
Then, rub hair dry with a towel.
Finally, comb hair.

b) First, switch on the grill.
At the same time, slice as much bread as you wish to toast.
Then, place the bread in the grill pan under the grill.
Brown both sides of the toast.
After this, switch the grill off.
Finally, butter the hot toast.

Exercise 4
A a) The *indicator* said that the petrol tank was empty.
  b) You carry a radio by its *handle*.
  c) Push the *button* to call the tutor.
  d) There are three light *switches* in the room.
  e) He tried all the *knobs* at the back of the TV set.
  f) There are two kinds of brake in a car: one of them works when you use a *lever*, the other one when you push down a *pedal*.

B a) When you make a radio louder you turn *it up*.
  b) When you don't want the radio on you switch *it off*.
  c) When you want to boil milk you put *it on the heat*.
  d) When you want cigarettes from a machine you push *a coin into the slot*.

4.1 Describing people

EXERCISES 1

Exercise 1
Hair: fair, auburn, nut-brown, dark, ginger, mousy (×), dull (×),
        curly, lank (×), frizzy, bobbed, long
Eyes: pale-green, hazel, dark, dull (×), almond-shaped, bloodshot (?), bright, large
Complexion: pale, fair, sallow, ruddy, dark, rosy, spotty (×), pasty (×)

Exercise 2

a) The round-*faced* man went through the door on his short, stumpy
legs. His long, *wavy* hair was an extraordinary reddy-*brown*
colour. His eyes were rather deep-*set* and light-*blue*. How square
and set his *jaw* was! How *broad* his shoulders! Only his long,
delicate, restless *fingers* modified this impression of determination.

b) These are possibilities:
The police are looking for a *black/blonde* etc. -haired girl with
grey-green *eyes*. Her *eyelashes* and *eyebrows* are *black/blonde* etc.
like her hair. She is rather pale in *complexion*; the face is *oval*. She
is very *slim*, almost thin, and about 5 foot 3 inches *tall*. She has
thin *lips* and a snub *nose*.

Exercise 3

Women's indoor:	a suit, a trouser-suit, a scarf, tights, a rollneck, a waistcoat, cords, overalls
Women's outdoor:	a duffle-coat, a scarf, a sweater, wellingtons, overalls
Men's indoor:	a suit, a dinner-jacket, a rollneck, a waistcoat, cords, overalls
Men's outdoor:	a duffle-coat, a scarf, a sweater, wellingtons, overalls

List A 1 The Queen dresses elegantly/formally.
2 Sunbathers dress scantily.
3 A hitchhiker is usually dressed casually/scruffily.
4 A wine-waiter dresses neatly/formally.
5 A bank manager dresses neatly/formally.
6 A bank manager dresses casually at home (even scruffily?).

Exercise 4

You probably have crosses against the following.

The woman: *skinny* is definitely uncomplimentary
slouches suggests a graceless way of walking
plump some women may find this uncomplimentary
though it isn't necessarily intended as an insult

The man: *short and squat* are both very uncomplimentary
B.O. – body odour – smells badly!
strides about some men may find this uncomplimentary

4.1 Describing people

EXERCISES 2

Exercise 1
Positive: bright (dull), brilliant (dull/stupid), sane (insane/mad), imaginative (unimaginative/staid), witty (humdrum/dull), brainy (thick/unintelligent)
Negative: silly (sensible), simple-minded (sophisticated/intelligent)
Neutral: naive (knowing/aware/sophisticated)

Exercise 2
Positive moral qualities: sincere/unselfish/patient/affectionate/fair/ trusting
Negative moral qualities: mean/callous/insensitive/devious/vain/cruel

(a) insensitive   (b) unselfish   (c) devious   (d) mean
(e) affectionate   (f) callous   (g) patient

Exercise 3
Your teacher will have to correct these sentences for you.

Exercise 4
(a) scowls   (b) laugh/frown/grimace   (c) frown   (d) pout and sulk
(e) grin/smile

4.2 Describing places

Exercise 1
a) in the western part of ...
b) ... north-west of ...
c) ... in the southern part ...
d) North of ... ... Southwards, ...
e) on the east ... ; south-west of ...
f) ... south-west ...

Exercise 2
a) ... right ...
b) ... opposite ...
c) ... between ...
d) ... next to ... , ... near ...

Exercise 3
Framley is a small town situated 15 miles east of Bladen. It has one famous *landmark*, the 19th century Town Hall, a popular *tourist attraction*, which is in the *centre* of the town. Most people live in the *suburbs*, in well-defined *residential areas*, and 50% work on the *industrial estate* by the *riverside*. Recently the town has adopted a *one-way-system* which confuses *residents* and *tourists* alike. A little way out of Framley on Bladen Height, there is a fine *view* over the whole *area*.

Exercise 4

The versions offered below are only some of many correct
possibilities.

A *The Town Hall* is situated in the *centre* of the town.

B *The Library* is *right next* to the Magistrates' Court.

C *The Magistrates' Court* has been built *along* Fore Street.

D *St Edmund's Church* is *not far* from the main civic buildings.

E *The Bus Station* is *on the corner* of The Hey and Warwick Road.

F *The Railway Station* is *to the south-east* of the River Wenge.

4.3   Describing objects

Exercise 1

measurements	long ... wide ... depth
weight and volume	weighs ... weight
	contains / holds
age	years old
colour	pink / red / orange
shape	heart- ... round ... oval
material	made of ... wooden
pattern	check ... striped ... plain
sensory	hollow / empty ... smooth ... sweet ... glossy / shiny
condition	worn out ... new
use	is used for
capacity	can be / may be

Exercise 2

3 – in the middle of the front side

4 – on the right-hand edge of the front side

5 – to the left-hand side of the top

6 – in the middle of the top

7 – in the middle of the front side, at the bottom

8 – in the bottom left-hand corner on the front; on the front, in the ...

Exercise 3

a) It's about 25 cm long   (length)

It's about 8 cm wide / in width   (width)

It's made of plastic and aluminium / steel / light metals   (materials)

b) They are semi-circular, and have a roughly cylindrical stem
with a round, slightly convex base   (shape)

They are wooden / made of wood   (material)

They feel smooth / grainy   (surface feel)

c) It weighs about 3 to 4 pounds (1½ to 2 kilos)   (weight)
    It is pinkish-red / red / reddy-brown / pink in colour   (colour)
    It is cylindrical   (shape)

d) It is 20 cm across / in diameter   (diameter)
    It holds 2 litres of water   (volume)
    It has a shiny surface   (surface look)

e) It is a hundred metres high   (height)
    It is 2 kilometres long   (length)
    It is used for carrying road transport across a river   (use)

f) It is made of steel, plastic, and other metals   (materials)
    It is seven metres long, two metres wide, and about a metre and a
        third high / one metre 40 centimetres high   (general size)

4.4   Describing human scenes

Exercise 1
The solutions below are not the only possible correct sentences.

A a) He's holding a heavy sack on his shoulder. He's waiting to load
       the shopping into the van.
   b) They have been shopping.
   c) I can see a large number of tins, jars and other goods.
   d) She's opening the door of the van. She's about to load the
       shopping into the van.
   e) They haven't put all the shopping into the van yet.
   f) The man has just said, 'Cor ... this is heavy!'

B a) They've been at school.
   b) They've been studying (or not) at school.
   c) They are playing about / playing conkers / playing games.
       They are enjoying themselves.
   d) One boy has just swung his conker; another boy is holding his
       conker up in the air.
   e) They haven't got home yet.

Exercise 2
It *is* really difficult to start this letter now because such a long time *has passed* since I left. Ever since my return to Germany I *have had* one thing in mind: to write to you. But up to now I *have not done* anything about it. So I *have had* to make myself do it, and this is the result. At present I *am working* in a factory all day until I get my chance to get into Lufthansa. I *have already found* that factory work *is boring* ...

157

Exercise 3

Ask your teacher to mark this exercise for you. The sentences below
are true sentences for the author – they are therefore model answers.
a) Rain is still falling in the street outside. The Christmas pudding is
   still steaming away in the saucepan.
b) I can hear somebody playing the piano.
c) My youngest daughter hasn't got up yet.
d) The children aren't eating at the moment.
e) I can't see any of my family from where I'm typing.
f) That candle has been burning since the early afternoon.
g) Ana and Lisa have already played three games of chess this
   morning.
h) Three people have come into the room in the last minute.

4.5   Describing landscape

Exercise 1

The river winds away into the *distance* and on the *horizon* is a line of
hills *silhouetted* against the distant *skyline*. There is a village in the
middle distance, *beyond* which there is a small wood. In the centre of
the village there is an old stone church *surrounded by* stone cottages.
Across the river lies the other half of the village. Half the scene is still
in bright *sunlight* and offers a glowing *view* of a Welsh country
village.

Exercise 2

1 a ploughed field	6 a line of hills
2 grazing land	7 a line/clump of trees
3 a pond	8 an orchard (fruit trees planted in one area)
4 a hedge	9 a haystack
5 a (wooden) fence	

Exercise 3

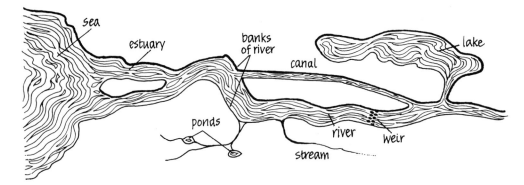

158

Exercise 4

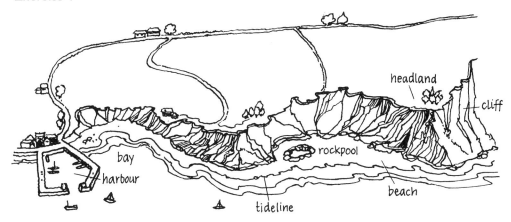

Exercise 5

A fast new *motorway* links Taunton and Exeter but there are also two
other *main roads* connecting the two main towns. Friends of mine live
a little way out of Exeter and to get there one must drive along a
twisting *country lane* for two miles. Another acquaintance of mine
works on a farm which is at the end of a bumpy dirt *track*. There are
plenty of *footpaths* across Dartmoor but always remember to close
the *gates* after you. There are also a number of *bridlepaths* for horse
riders in the foothills of Dartmoor. In Exeter itself there are a number
of curious old *alleyways* between the old stone buildings.

Exercise 6

There is a haze today
    a breeze today
    a mist today
    an overcast sky today
    a clear sky today
    a cloudless sky today
    a wintry sky today

It is a clear day today
    cloudless day today
    dull day today
    wintry day today
    muggy day today

It is overcast today
    clear today
    dull today
    muggy today
    drizzling today

Exercise 7

√ spectacular	× melancholy
charming	dull
stirring	dismal
picturesque	depressing
breath-taking	
pretty	

a) spectacular/stirring/breath-taking (because of the large scale)
b) charming/picturesque/pretty/depressing (if a dying village)

4.6   Describing habits and conditions

Exercise 1   Versions in brackets are acceptable but less common.
a) He watches TV every day.   (Every day he watches TV.)
b) They never phone me.
c) She never ever eats with her fingers.
d) Once a week I have a sauna. *or* I have a sauna once a week.
e) The British seldom eat good fish.
f) It frequently rains in London.
g) It doesn't generally snow in Devon.
h) We almost always have a holiday in August.
i) They play a lot of chess on Mondays. (On Mondays they play a lot of chess.)
j) I see my mother somewhat infrequently.   (Somewhat infrequently I see my mother.)

Exercise 2
e.g. My brother has the irritating habit of playing his record player very loudly.
Ask your teacher to check this exercise for you.

4.7   Describing processes

Exercise 1   These are model answers only.
c) Patients are treated by the medical staff.
d) Some patients become worse.
e) Some patients are given blood transfusions.
f) Some patients die.
g) Patients are carefully nursed by the nursing staff.
h) Patients are visited by relatives and friends.
i) Some patients get well again.
j) Patients are examined by doctors.
k) Some patients only seem ill.

Exercise 2   These are model answers only.
b) *Cement* is mixed and used to construct buildings and walls.
c) *An old battery* is thrown away/replaced by a new one.
d) *A poor footballer* is sacked/dropped.
e) *An old language laboratory* is replaced by a new one.
f) *Fish* are caught and eaten, after being cooked.
g) *Coffee beans* are ground.
h) *A criminal* is arrested, charged and sent to prison.

Exercise 3
'... the sugar *is added* and the jam soon *turns* thick. Once it *becomes/has become* thick enough to stand a spoon in, it *is poured* into pound jam-jars. As soon as it *has cooled* a cellophane disc *is placed* on the surface of the jam and the jars *are sealed* with more cellophane and rubber bands. The jam *deteriorates* the longer you keep it so it *is normally eaten* within a year of being made ...'

Exercise 4
There are different solutions to this exercise. Check with your teacher if you have written different sentences from the ones here.
a) Contact was made by telephone.
b) Goods are moved using railways.
c) Grapes are picked with the help of local people and students.
d) Cars are lifted through the use of jacks.
e) Doors are opened by means of keys.
f) Preserving, involving salting and freezing, is an important part of most cooking traditions.

Exercise 5

Making Bread   There are four separate stages in making bread. The first stage begins by mixing yeast with warm water. This mixture is then added to half the amount of flour. The resultant batter mixture is then left for an hour. At the next stage the rest of the flour is added to the risen batter mixture, along with salt and oil. The main step in the second stage is a thorough kneading of the dough, after which it is left to rise. The third stage involves shaping the dough into loaves; the shaped loaves are then put into bread tins and left to 'prove' (rise). In the final stage the bread is cooked in a hot oven. The whole process of bread-making finishes when the bread is taken from the oven and left to cool on wire racks.

5.1 *Reporting incidents and events*

Exercise 1

a) had been talking (possible –
     were talking), arrived
b) happened
c) popped in
d) had never eaten

e) saw him
f) were laughing
g) had been smoking
h) was watching

Exercise 2

As soon as I got home, my brother *rushed* out of the kitchen. This *was* surprising because he *had only done* this once before. Up to this day my brother *had always* (been) slumped in his chair at six, watching the news. So what *was* special this particular night? Well, sometime earlier in the day he *had found* a job! Apparently, five minutes before he *was* due to turn up at the local Job Centre, an old friend *had rung* him up to ask if he *wanted* a job sailing ferries for the summer. He *had said* 'yes', of course. So he *had been* busy for the rest of the afternoon, getting his things in order. If he *had gone* out earlier to the Job Centre, he would have missed the call and probably *wouldn't have got* the job.

Exercise 3

The sentences given below can only serve as models. Ask your teacher to check your sentences.

a) People stare at that lady whenever *she appears in public.*
b) When Mandy told me about her father's death, *she got very upset.*
c) David phoned the hospital as soon as *he (had) heard about Tony's accident.*
d) After he had visited the old lady, *he went home.*
e) I learned to speak before *I could write.*
f) My landlady goes to bed directly *the TV news programme comes to an end.*
g) Immediately the doorbell rang, *Geoff jumped up to answer it.*
h) As long as you don't overwork, *you should remain fit and healthy.*
i) I haven't seen Herman since *I lent him five pounds a fortnight ago.*
j) He was able to speak fairly good Spanish once *he had lived in the country for six months.*
k) The moment that he left school, my father *started work in a surveyor's office.*
l) She refused to speak to me until *she felt quite well and recovered from her journey.*
m) Every time I go to France, *I buy a whole Camembert.*
n) He phoned her every day while *he was travelling round Scotland.*
o) You should speak good English now that *you've been here nine months.*

5.3 Narrating

This is the original continuation of the story on page 90 in the
Student's Book.

RUNAWAY

It had been very easy to get away. They were used to her getting up and
moving around the house at 5 o'clock in the morning. She knew that she
would be long gone before they even got out of bed. She had packed her bags
the night before and was ready to go in half an hour. The bus driver had been
a bit of a problem. He was a cheeky youth with a crew cut hairdo.

'Running away from home are you missus?' he called down the bus to her
as she struggled in the gangway with her bags. Lucky there was no one else
on the bus at that time of the morning.

As they drove through the empty suburbs she worked out her finances. She
had ten pounds and fifty pence plus an uncashed pension cheque for
twenty-eight pounds thirty two. She decided that this much would keep her
in food and rent for about a week. There was a lot to be done in just one day.
She had to find a room, visit the labour exchange, or job centre as they called
them these days, and cash her cheque at the post office. After getting off the
bus she went straight to the railway station and studied the newspaper over a
cup of tea. For the first time she began to worry about what she had done.
She had assumed that the amount of rent you paid would be lower if you did
your own cooking and cleaning and bought your own food. The rooms
advertised in the paper were nearly twice what she paid Janice, just for a
single room.

She had also begun to feel guilty. It was eight o'clock. The family would be
up by now, wondering why the tea wasn't made. They would all be late. But
she was determined to be independent, and made her way to the job centre.
Everyone was hurrying to work. People had begun to arrive at the job centre.
Most already looked weary; all were young. The room was full of boards
with cards on them, like a tobacconist's window. Mary approached a young
girl sitting at a desk at the end of the office.

'Excuse me, miss. Have you got any part-time jobs in the tailoring line? I'm
a seamstress by trade.' The girl looked at first as if she had not understood
but then smiled and excused herself. Mary could see her talking to a man in a
glass office. Both glanced in her direction several times before the man
nodded and took a piece of paper out of a drawer. He came towards her,
smiling.

'Good morning, madam. Miss Allen tells me you're looking for a part-time
job as a seamstress.'

Mary nodded and searched in her handbag. 'Yes, that's right. I have
references.'

The man held up his hand to stop her. 'Well, I'm afraid we don't have
anything at the moment for part-time work, but if you'll give me your name
and address perhaps we could contact you later.' He pushed the paper
towards her.

Mary was horrified. What could she say? That she was homeless? She
blushed at the thought of 'no fixed abode'.

As she hurried away from the office Mary realised that they thought she was too old! It seemed that she was too old to have a job which paid enough for her to live independently, but young enough to work all day looking after her daughter's family for nothing.

The nine o'clock rush had finished and Mary felt more at ease with her aimlessness. She found herself heading naturally towards the shopping area; the part of the city she knew best. She was surprised to find the shops nearly deserted. She had never been to town on a Monday morning before. She and Janice always did the shopping on Friday nights, pushing through the crowds, hanging on to the children.

She caught her reflection in a shop window. It was something she had never noticed before. A small shuffling figure, slightly hunched in an old coat reaching almost to her ankles. She made an effort to look away but her gaze was constantly drawn to meet that of the old woman in the glass. It had begun to rain. She felt the rain on her head through her wispy grey hair. Once it was long and thick; too thick to feel the rain through. Now each drop touched her scalp and rolled down following the wrinkles of her face and neck.

She passed the time looking at clothes, thinking how they might look on Janice, Barbara or the little girls. At lunchtime she had a cup of tea on a high stool in a snack bar. Usually when they had lunch in a cafe, she looked after the bags while Janice bought the food. It was too hard to manage on her own.

She was very tired and her legs ached from walking aimlessly along the pavements. Her bags were so heavy that she had to keep stopping to rest her arms. Soon the street filled again with the home-bound crowds and she was jostled and pushed aside by them.

Somehow she arrived at the park and sat, probably for hours, as the afternoon became evening and the drizzle became heavy rain. The footsteps were getting louder, definitely coming towards her in the dark. A woman's face suddenly appeared under the light of a lamp post, then disappeared again in the darkness, to reappear under the next lamp post. As she came closer, Mary could see it was Janice. She was both relieved and afraid; glad and miserable.

There was silence for a moment as Janice surveyed her mother. 'Barbara's pretty mad at having to stay at home with the kids, you know,' she said, not unkindly, 'She and Ken were going to go to the pictures tonight.' Mary nodded without looking up.

'Come on Mum.' Janice took Mary's arm and helped her to her feet, taking the bags in her other hand, 'Doug said he'd wait for us in the car by the War Memorial.' She continued to guide the old lady down the path.

'I suppose you've caught your death of cold in that old coat haven't you? I don't know why you won't let me buy you a new one.'

5.4 *Reporting speech*

Exercise 1

a) She stated that marriage was still important.
b) She claimed that it had many enemies.

c) She suggested that, as women's roles changed, marriage was becoming less easy.
d) She said that marital roles had begun to change.
e) She added that they would change further of course.
f) She stated that women would still be having babies in 50 years' time.
g) She denied that marriage could possibly disappear.
h) She explained that it had begun from necessity.
i) She continued that it was going to remain from necessity.

Exercise 2
a) He said (that) he didn't like him.
b) He asked me if I did.
c) He asked me if I wanted a drink.   or   He offered me a drink.
d) She told me she had never drunk alcohol.
    or   She denied she had ever drunk any alcohol.
e) She told me that he wouldn't drink with her.
f) She asked me if/whether it was immoral.
g) He asked me if I could explain that.
h) She asked me where I had been / was born.
i) She said she mightn't come.
j) He asked (me) if I had finished.
k) She asked (me) what he had done.
l) She said (that) she wouldn't have to work if she stayed in England.

Exercise 3
The boss *asked* if we had any ideas. I *suggested* that we should reduce the number of staff. He *revealed* that this had been done already, but *added* he didn't really like this. Robin then *spoke* and seemed to *imply* that the only hope was to expand. He *claimed* we hadn't expanded for five years.

7.1 Paragraph writing

EXERCISES 1

These are suggested answers to the exercise. Your teacher will have to check your own ideas.

1 The paragraph is about the decreasing interest of the British in trade and industry in the nineteenth century.
   Main sentence: First part of the first sentence.

2 The paragraph is about the take-over of British firms by foreign owners after the Second World War.
   Main sentence: The last sentence of the paragraph; but possibly the first one as well.

3 The paragraph is about the position of Indians in a foreign society. The main sentence is the first one.

4 The paragraph is about the quality and character of British television.
Main sentence: The second part of the first sentence 'and British television soon began to reflect the traditions of its people.'

5 The paragraph is about the author's changed feelings about sugarcane.
The main sentence: A sentence in the middle of the paragraph 'Now, in the uneven land of central and south Trinidad, I saw that even sugarcane could be beautiful.'

6 This paragraph is about the necessity of controlling the strong emotion of anger.
Main sentence: The first sentence sets the paragraph off, but the fifth sentence partially repeats the idea contained in the first sentence.

7 This paragraph is about the nature of the independence achieved by a mature woman. All the sentences in this paragraph are about this idea, but there is no single main sentence since each sentence deals with different aspects of the unexpressed theme: dependence, self-esteem, the esteem of others, emotional and intellectual independence.

EXERCISES 2

In both exercises, the answers suggested below can only serve as models. You must ask your teacher to check your work.

Exercise 1

Boots   A boot is a watertight item of footwear that covers the foot and part of the leg. Farmers, fishermen, children and adults all wear boots for one reason or another. Some merely wish to keep their feet and legs dry while working or playing in wet conditions; others wear them to look good. I, personally, wear boots only when gardening in muddy weather.

Income Tax   Income tax is money collected by central government from the money that people earn. It is collected either as people earn it, or at the end of a calendar period. Most people resent paying income tax.

Vegetarianism   Vegetarianism is the use of a diet that avoids using meat, and sometimes fish, cheese, eggs, and milk as well. Some people follow such a diet because they don't wish to cause suffering to

animals. Others believe that a meat-free diet is healthier for the body.
I suspect that it is difficult to sustain a consistent argument on moral
grounds but that it is quite easy to offer convincing evidence that our
diets would be healthier if we ate less meat or no meat at all.

Exercise 2

Make-up   Make-up is creams, powders and oils applied to the body (1).
It is generally applied to the face, but it can be used on any part of
the body (1a). Some people use small amounts, such as a light lipstick,
or face powder while others cake the face and body in heavy make-up
in ways which transform the features (1b). In Western society it is
usually adult women who wear make-up (2). However make-up is
also widely used in the performing arts: theatre, television, and
opera (2a). It is also used by detectives and criminal investigators, or
by criminals wishing to escape detection (2b). People use make-up in
order to change their appearance for some reason (3). For example,
women apply pinkish face powders to appear more 'blooming' than
they actually are (3a). Similarly, a man may apply face powder to
cover an outbreak of acne (3b). In the theatre, make-up is used to
make very young actors appear very old and vice versa (3c). In real
life it seems a pity that people feel that they have to obscure their
natural self and project an alternative image through the use of
make-up (4).

7.3   Practice 1 *(from Student's Book)*

There is never a 'correct' summary of any piece of information. Talk
to your teacher about anything in these model summaries you
disagree with.

A You can patch toddlers' worn dungarees cheaply and attractively
with washable cloth book pages.

B Princess Anne's refusal to respond to the greeting of a young child
while on a televised charity visit to an Oslo hospital this weekend
has shocked many Norwegians. Norwegian newspapers say they
were contacted by thousands of people objecting to the princess's
unmotherly behaviour, and also suggesting she went home. A
British spokesman, however, said that the incident had been seen
out of context and had given the wrong impression.

7.3 Practice 2 *(from Student's Book)*

Talk to your teacher about your summaries and how they differ from the versions below.

A Showing short 'safety' films in the cinema would be an excellent way of promoting awareness of the need for everyday 'safety consciousness'.

B It seems very unfair that women who find it essential to work can't claim tax allowances for the wages of necessary child-minders in the way that you can, for example, for looking after an elderly relative.
   Although full-time care in state nurseries may be available for the under-5s, child-minding for school-age children can cost £10 a week. Au pairs, though cheaper, are not always a reliable solution; and allowing the children to remain uncared for after school is both emotionally and socially undesirable. For some, however, this is the only solution.

7.3 Practice 3 *(from Student's Book)*

A Kate accused Paul of over-using salt on his food, arguing that this was both unhealthy and also disguised the real flavours of food. Paul disagreed saying that he was very healthy and that salt brought out flavour rather than masked it and that some foods wouldn't taste at all without the addition of salt.

B Mr Whitelaw reported to the House of Commons that Mr Dellow's inquiry had revealed that the security problems at Buckingham Palace had been the result of police negligence at several levels and that all those responsible or involved had now resigned, been suspended or transferred. In the interests of justice to those involved, Mr Whitelaw refused to say more.

7.3 Extra practice 1

A Do not enter details about what you earn from your main job. Enter full details of your wife's job and her earnings after superannuation has been deducted. Enter full details and the total of *all* other earnings by you and your wife before any deductions. Enter the total amount of tips and perks received from all sources including details of accommodation if this is one of the perks.

B AIRSHIPWRECK
A well-illustrated account of the unfamiliar but fascinating events
of the pioneering age of the airship.

AVIATION: AN ILLUSTRATED HISTORY
An extensively-illustrated technical history of the world's great
aircraft.

CATHEDRALS IN BRITAIN AND IRELAND
A fully-illustrated description of all the Pre-Reformation British
cathedrals including historical information.

THE HISTORY OF SHIPS
A pictorial history of ships accompanied by appropriate
informational accounts.

7.3   Extra practice 2

A Cheap tall gladioli bulbs/plants of various colours for garden or house.

Cheap unusually beautiful shorter gladioli bulbs in a variety of
colours, for garden or decoration.

B 'Professionalisation' is a series of five inexpensive weekend courses
between March and June designed to increase professional
expertise for administrators in arts organisations about aspects of
arts promotion. They are run by South West Arts and City
University (financially aided by the Arts Council) who will arrange
the venues. If you want to be one of the 35 participants for any
course, apply to John de la Cour at South West Arts immediately.

7.3   Extra practice 3

A In this talk Patricia Ruanne said that she'd go on dancing for as
long as she could, until people told her that she was no longer any
good. She wasn't worried about this because she felt she still had a
number of years dancing left to her. After that, since she couldn't
do anything else, she would take minor and character parts. This
would be difficult but she would find it interesting – lots of other
ballerinas don't – and she had already begun to learn such parts.

B Upon inquiry, the cyclist informed the motorist that he had injured
his left leg. He blamed the motorist for running into him from
behind after failing to see him. The motorist disputed this and
blamed the cyclist in turn for stopping suddenly without signalling
properly before turning right.

7.3 Test 1

These are only possible summaries. There is no one correct version.

A Professor Hans Reuter has found some proof for the common belief that garlic has medicinal properties by showing that the herb can reduce cholesterol levels in people who eat too much fatty food and thus lessen the risk of heart problems. In experiments where volunteers were fed both fatty foods and fresh garlic (not processed garlic) or just garlic, cholesterol levels fell significantly after a month. It also killed off dangerous disease bacteria sometimes better than penicillin.

B HMS Bristol, whether at sea anywhere in the world or in port, provides a 'home' for officers and a highly-trained crew. While numerous mechanical aids to help the crew control the ship take up much space, the remaining space provides a comfortable, modern living area to sleep, work, eat and play in. Inevitably, both men and facilities on HMS Bristol are expensive.

7.3 Test 2

A The best example of working British Democratic Socialism was in the Second World War because Britain used her resources to employ everyone without exception, to produce a lot, to mobilise effectively, to pay high pensions and benefits, and to look after those in difficulty. The common, democratic aim broke down class barriers, seemingly for ever. Since then they have been rebuilt and our policies are the reverse of wartime ones and have damaged us.

B John and Linda lost 7 and 4 stones respectively by eating and drinking less, and by changing their diet to more nutritious food. This won them £1,000 in a slimming competition and, best of all, improved their sex life.